# Mrs Bridges' Upstairs Downstairs Cookery Book

EDITED BY ADRIAN BAILEY
WITH PHOTOGRAPHS BY JOHN HEDGECOE

*Simon and Schuster*
*New York*

Published by Simon and Schuster
Rockefeller Center, 630 Fifth Avenue
New York, New York 10020

Manufactured in the United States of America
1  2  3  4  5  6  7  8  9  10

Library of Congress Cataloging in Publication Data
Bridges, Kate.
Mrs Bridges' upstairs, downstairs cookery book.
"Originally published in 1905 under the title
Practical household cookery."
Includes index.
1. Cookery, English.   I. Bailey, Adrian, 1928-
ed.   II. Title.
TX717.B74    1975      641.5′942      74-32163
ISBN  0-671-22029-2
ISBN  0-671-22030-6  pbk.

## *Foreword from the original book*

'I began collecting receipts when I was under-cook to Mrs Harcourt, a fine cook in the French fashion, at Southwold in Wiltshire. Mrs Harcourt, who came from Sussex, also taught me to prepare some of her own family receipts. I remember my mother, who was a Bedfordshire woman, teaching me some country dishes which she had learned, and have never before been written down. She too was a good cook, in the ways of the country.

While in the service of Lady Marjorie Bellamy, I prepared dinners and banquets for the famous, which Mr Bellamy has kindly permitted me to mention. I was very proud to cook a dinner for no less a personage than King Edward himself!

I owe a great debt to Lady Marjorie, who first suggested that I put my collection of receipts into a book, in the manner of the well-known Mrs Beeton; and to Miss Elizabeth Bellamy, who helped me in its preparation. I hope that the receipts will serve the needs of cooks and of hostesses for the many and varied occasions throughout the seasons.'

1905                                  Kate Bridges,
                                      165 Eaton Place,
                                      London, SW1

# CONTENTS

The Bellamys' home at 165 Eaton Place, London, where Mrs Bridges
wrote her cookery book during the early 1900's.

# Editor's Introduction

The *Upstairs, Downstairs Cookery Book* was originally published in 1905 under the title *Practical Household Cookery* by K. Bridges, and subtitled 'Popular dishes for Town and Country Houses'. Its author, Kate Bridges, received her training under Lady Marjorie Bellamy's cook, Mrs Harcourt, at Southwold House in Wiltshire. Mrs Harcourt had been a pupil at Marshall's Cookery School in Mortimer Street in London, and later worked with one of Escoffier's chefs at the Carlton Hotel.

*Practical Household Cookery* was a collection of favourite recipes, and also contained many valuable observations and practical information about Edwardian domestic life. It was one of the first books to give menus both for the 'Household' and the 'Kitchen' – Upstairs and Downstairs, in fact.

Apart from the well-known English dishes, there was a large proportion from the repertoire of French *haute cuisine*, so popular with the Edwardian upper class, slightly simplified for the amateur cook. The book was written at 165 Eaton Place, London, the Bellamys' town residence, and published by Godstone & Ryland. Except in her acknowledgements in the Foreword, Mrs Bridges is careful to omit any reference to her employers. To have done so would have contravened Edwardian privacy and privilege.

Mrs Bridges acknowledges Mrs Beeton in her Foreword, and obviously had her illustrious predecessor's book in mind when writing her own. Mrs Bridges' book, however, is the smaller of the two, but still too long by today's demands to publish in its entirety. The difference between Mrs Bridges and Mrs Beeton was, quite simply, one of class. Mrs Bridges was a countrywoman and a cook; Mrs Beeton was also a cook, an expert on domestic science – and the wife of a famous publisher. Mrs Bridges writes as from one cook to another, whereas Mrs Beeton was more inclined to write to the mistress of the house. Mrs Bridges sometimes strays away from the kitchen on faintly autobiographical paths, but we learn little about the real Mrs Beeton from the mighty *Household Management*, or from *Everyday Cookery*.

Mrs Bridges was primarily an English cook, using the best of ingredients as simply as possible, and quite a few recipes selected for the *Upstairs, Downstairs Cookery Book* could have been placed equally well in either section. 'From all my years in service I have learned that gentlemen and menservants alike share a preference for pies, cold cuts and pickles, when all is said and done.'

Unfortunately, very few copies of Mrs Bridges' original book have survived, even though it was reprinted four times. Godstone & Ryland went bankrupt just after World War I, and efforts to trace their collection have failed. The British Museum's only copy was destroyed in the blitz, and the one surviving copy was discovered in a bookshop in Petersfield, Hampshire, in 1960.

Kate Bridges was born in Bristol, but her mother came from Sandy, in Bedfordshire, and so we find an inheritance of local recipes. There are references to cheeses from Cambridge, cheeses now extinct; harvest beer and cakes from Bedfordshire; rook pie from Wiltshire, Sally Lunns and Bath buns from the West Country, Mrs Bridges' home. For the *Upstairs, Downstairs Cookery Book*, recipes have been brought up to date, using ingredients more practical to today's demands, and giving oven temperatures; there was no regulator on Mrs Bridges' kitchen range, ovens were either 'quick', 'moderate', or 'slow'.

Throughout the book we have tried to preserve some of Mrs Bridges' original, and often caustic, observations. 'Chocolate cake,' she writes, 'must *never* be flavoured with anything other than vanilla. Some cooks *ruin* good chocolate cake by adding grated orange peel, or rum, or even coffee!' Times have changed. There were few refrigerators at the turn of the century, and Mrs Bridges' Champagne Sorbet would have been stirred over quantities of ice. Food was cooked on a coal range, and mostly on top of the stove, for this was the age of the boiled and steamed puddings, for which Mrs Bridges gave no fewer than one hundred and sixty recipes!

To reprint Mrs Bridges' original book – there were nearly a thousand pages – would have been both expensive and impracticable, while an edited version ensures that Mrs Bridges reaches a far wider public than she can ever have imagined. I have selected the most acceptable recipes to modern taste, and have included a few curiosities. Some recipes have been abbreviated, especially where Mrs Bridges was inclined to be rather long-winded or, as she herself would have put it – 'painstaking'. Where short cuts were possible, we took them, yet trying to preserve the flavour of the solid, bourgeois Edwardian kitchen. There is no doubt that Mrs Bridges was an excellent cook, nor are her observations on the art of cookery, written nearly seventy years ago, any less true today.

# WEIGHTS & MEASURES

## SOLID

| By Weight | By Equivalent Measure |
|---|---|
| ½ ounce | 1 tablespoon (3 teaspoons) |
| 2 ounces | ¼ cup (4 tablespoons) |
| 4 ounces | ½ cup (8 tablespoons) |
| 8 ounces (½ pound) | 1 cup |
| 16 ounces (1 pound) | 2 cups |
| 32 ounces (2 pounds) | 4 cups |

*Note:* The above table shows the approximate weights, per standard measurement, of most common ingredients—granulated sugar, butter, lard, rice, etc. Very light ingredients (flour, cornmeal, powdered white sugar, etc.) will weigh roughly half as much per standard measurement. For example, 4 cups of granulated sugar will weigh 2 pounds, as shown in the table, but 4 cups of flour will weigh only about 1 pound.

## LIQUID

*(All American fluid measurements, such as gills, pints, quarts and gallons, are only ⅘ of their English name equivalents.)*

| English Liquid Measure | American Equivalent |
|---|---|
| ½ pint (10 fluid ounces) | 1¼ cups |
| 1 pint (20 fluid ounces) | 2½ cups |
| 1 quart (40 fluid ounces) | 5 cups |
| 1 gallon | 5 quarts |

# NOTE ON
# THE RECIPES

For the *Upstairs, Downstairs Cookery Book*, Mrs Bridges' original recipes have been simplified or abbreviated. As her recipes show, she assumed that her work would serve those cooks, both amateur and professional, who knew the rudiments of cooking, or indeed were considerably advanced in kitchen techniques. Here is one of her recipes, reprinted from the original:

### Éclairs au Café

'Prepare a choux paste and put it in a forcing bag. Force it out on an ungreased baking tin, so that you have éclairs which are four inches long and three-quarters of an inch in thickness. Brush your éclairs with a well-beaten whole egg. Put them to bake for about half an hour, until they have taken on a delicate golden colour. Split them down one side on removing from the oven, so that steam may escape, otherwise the paste will become limp. When they are cold, fill them with French pastry cream, or with fresh whipped cream, flavoured or not as you wish with coffee. Coat the top of each éclair with coffee *glacé* icing. Dish them on a pretty napkin or lace dish-paper.'

Although quantities were nearly always given, oven temperatures were not, and the sizes of cake tins and moulds were omitted. For the *Upstairs, Downstairs Cookery Book*, Mrs Bridges' recipes have been either tested or interpreted. Included are several everyday, familiar recipes, many perhaps less familiar,

many that are cheap to make, others expensive – and some that are novelties – her Tea Soufflé, for example.

Throughout this book, oven temperatures are given in degrees Fahrenheit, and the equivalent Gas setting is as follows:

| Fahrenheit | Gas | | |
|---|---|---|---|
| 250 | $\frac{1}{2}$ | Very slow oven | |
| 275 | 1 | Slow | |
| 300 | 2 | ,, | |
| 325 | 3 | ,, | |
| 350 | 4 | Moderate (good temperature for cakes) | |
| 375 | 5 | ,, | |
| 400 | 6 | ,, | |
| 425 | 7 | Hot, or 'Quick' | (425 & 450 for bread |
| 450 | 8 | Very hot | and certain kinds of pastry) |
| 475–500 | 9 | Very hot | |

Finally, a few words of wisdom from Mrs Bridges' *Practical Household Cookery*:

'A newly-tried recipe should always be perfected in the kitchen. Cooks must become familiar with dishes before including them in the repertoire. Furthermore, cooks should always read a recipe through several times, so that one has forehand knowledge of the ingredients and methods of preparation. Well begun is half done.'

15

# STOCKS AND SAUCES

In the early 1900s the fashion of serving French dishes reflected the tastes and the extreme wealth of the upper classes, who followed the example set by the epicurean Edward VII. Very few of these dishes bore much resemblance to the real *grande cuisine*, which by the turn of the century had reached the heights of perfection, as well as eccentricity. Cooks like Mrs Bridges would have had neither the time nor the experience to produce the flamboyant *pièces de résistance* inspired by the great chef Carême.

But on a more simple level Mrs Bridges excelled, and she was the first to tell us so. 'Good French cooking,' she declared, 'needs practice and patience more than truffles and *foie gras*.' And with a nod to Victorian homilies, added, 'Experience leads the way to perfection.'

The art of making fine sauces was the foundation of French cuisine, to which were added those basic ingredients upon which the repertoire was founded: truffles, *foie gras*, pastry, and aspics. The truffles used at Eaton Place were bought in tins from Messrs Fortnum & Mason, as was the *foie gras* and the caviar, which came in china pots. If Mrs Bridges' Sauce Perigueux were not quite of the standard expected in France, it would have required far more discerning palates than those gathered round the table at Eaton Place to detect that the truffles were tinned.

In truth, Mrs Bridges' most receptive audience at Eaton Place was the staff and its employers who, when the dinner parties were over, turned to the more simple pleasures. They much preferred good gravy to Sauce Espagnole, custard to Sauce Sabayon, Parsley Sauce to Béarnaise. They were connoisseurs of Harvey's Sauce and Lea & Perrins' Worcestershire Sauce, of Mint Sauce and Mustard, Horseradish and Cumberland Rum Butter. We know that they were because Mrs Bridges says so. 'I have never made a sauce that was more acceptable than that which comes in a bottle,' she laments, 'such as Tomato Ketchup. Yet if I couldn't make a good Espagnole I would never call myself a cook.' And with a further acknowledgement to Victorian wisdom, adds, 'Anyway, as we all know, 'tis hunger that makes the best sauce.'

Aged chefs shake their heads and grumble that the decline of *grande cuisine* began when Espagnole Sauce went out of fashion. But few diners noticed that this brown foundation sauce had been superseded by something called *fonds lié*; only a connoisseur was able to detect the difference, like an art collector who discovers his Corot is a fake.

*Fonds lié* is stock reduced and thickened with arrowroot. It can be prepared in less than thirty minutes, and is the basis of many sauces. *Espagnole*, on the other hand, is brown veal stock, thickened with flour and cooked with vegetables for many hours. Reduced and concentrated, it was called a *demi-glace*, and was considered the apogee of the *saucier's* art. Today, a *demi-glace* is more or less the same thing as *fonds lié*. But Mrs Bridges was obliged to make Espagnole.

Very simply, the steps to making a sauce are as follows: You make a stock with veal and beef bones. It must simmer for twelve hours, so it is worth making in quantity and freezing for future use. This preparation is known as a *fond de veau*, and if preferred it can be coloured with commercial gravy browning or caramel, a practice that would make some chefs go rigid with shock. If you reduce a *fond de veau* to the consistency of syrup, you have a *glace de viande*, which is a kitchen version of commercial Marmite, and used to strengthen and augment certain sauces. This preparation is also known as a *fumet*, a term more frequently applied to a concentration of fish stock.

Short cuts can be taken by methods of which many cooks pretend ignorance. Bottled or tinned consommé can, for example, be used in place of stock, but it is likely to be rather salty if reduced. It can be thickened with a roux, or with arrowroot, or serve as the base of a brown *chaudfroid* sauce, or in place of aspic jelly if fortified by gelatine. Many a dish found its way upstairs in Eaton Place, where the sauce owed its deep brown colour and flavour to Oxo or Marmite. But whether Mrs Bridges tricked the French Ambassador's palate with Bisto is never disclosed.

Mr de Blank of Elizabeth Street the supplier of high-class provisions to Eaton Place.

# STOCKS AND SAUCES

## The Upstairs &
## Downstairs Recipes

Fond Brun de Veau  
Fonds Lié or Demi-glace  
Aspic  
Béarnaise  
Béchamel  
Bigarrade  
Bread  
Champagne  
Châteaubriand  
Chaudfroid  
Choron  
Cumberland  

Custard  
Gooseberry  
Hollandaise  
Horseradish  
Madère  
Mayonnaise  
Mornay  
Mustard  
Parsley  
Périgueux  
Port Wine  
Zingara

# Fond Brun de Veau

This stock can be used for sauces, aspics, soups and consommés. Reduced, it makes a *glace de viande*.

5 *lb veal and beef marrow and shin bones sawn in pieces*
½ *lb carrots*
2 *turnips*
2 *leeks*
1 *onion*

5 *sticks celery*
*bouquet garni, clove of garlic, 2 cloves, 2 bay leaves, 6 peppercorns*
6 *pints water*
2 *tablespoons oil*

Fry the vegetables, cleaned, peeled and sliced, except the onion, in oil for about 30 minutes, until they are brown. Put the bones with the whole onion in a roasting pan, and bake in the oven at 400° for 30 minutes. Both operations can be carried out together. Add the bones to the vegetables in a large pan with a capacity of about 12 pints. Stick the cloves in the onion, add the bouquet garni, the bay leaves, peppercorns and the water, and put on a low heat. Scum begins to rise to the surface in 20 minutes, and you will need to skim for about half an hour until all the scum has cleared. The stock should cook so slowly that only a gentle movement tells that it is cooking at all. On no account let it boil, as this may result in a cloudy stock, which is very difficult to clear. Part cover the pan, and leave to simmer for 10–12 hours, carefully adding more water if needed. Allow the stock to cool before straining through a cloth in a sieve into a large bowl. Leave to get completely cold before removing any fat on the surface. It is unlikely that this stock will need clarifying. It should be clear and brown, but should you wish to clear it, proceed as follows: Pour the stock into a pan, holding back any sediment that may have precipitated. Add the whites of 2 eggs, stiffly whipped, for every 3 pints of stock, plus the crushed eggshells. Bring slowly to the boil, whisking now and then. When at boiling-point, a crust will form on the surface. Remove from the heat and allow to settle for 5 minutes. Repeat the process without whisking, and leave for 10 minutes. Strain through a cloth into a bowl. If the stock is not clear and bright, repeat the process, but the stock must be cold before you do.

NB. White veal stock, for white sauces, is made in the same way, except that no previous browning of meat, bones and vegetables is required.

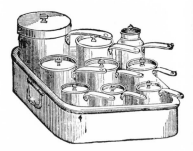

# Fonds Lié (or *demi-glace*)

1 *pint fond brun de veau*
1 *small onion*
1 *small carrot*
1 *stick of celery*
1 *teaspoon tomato purée*
2 *oz mushrooms*

2 *heaped tablespoons*
   *arrowroot*
*a bouquet garni, comprising*
   1 *bay leaf, a sprig of*
   *thyme and parsley*
*salt and pepper*

Finely dice all the vegetables, and fry them in butter until they lightly colour. The less butter you can use for this process the better. Add the *fond brun* and bouquet garni and cook for 20 minutes. Mix the arrowroot to a paste with cold water, and add the tomato purée. Add some stock to the paste, stirring well, and pour back into the pan. Season to taste and cook for about 10 minutes, or until the sauce begins to thicken. If a darker colour is required, a little caramel colouring may be added.

NB. Sauces, if left to cool, will form a skin on the surface which is tricky to remove. There are two methods of overcoming this. One is to cover the surface of the sauce with melted butter. The other classic method is simply to stir the sauce continuously with a wooden spoon until it is cold, so that no skin can form.

# Aspic Jelly

The simplest way to prepare aspic is to use powdered gelatine. With veal stock you will require about $1\frac{1}{2}$ oz to every 2 pints of liquid, but manufacturer's instructions are given with each packet. Aspics are improved with the addition of vinegar, lemon juice, sherry, white wine and other flavourings. Make sure your stock is clear and completely free of grease or fat.

# Béarnaise

8 *tablespoons wine vinegar*
2 *tablespoons finely chopped*
  *shallots or onion*
10 *peppercorns*
1 *bay leaf*
1 *blade of mace*

2 *teaspoons each of chopped*
  *parsley and tarragon*
5 *egg yolks*
5 *oz unsalted butter*
*salt*
*fresh chopped parsley and*
  *tarragon*

Boil the vinegar with the shallots, peppercorns, bay, mace, parsley and tarragon until reduced to 2 tablespoons of liquid. Beat the egg yolks in a bowl, strain the herb vinegar into the eggs. Cook in a double boiler or *bain-marie* over a gentle heat until the sauce begins to thicken, but do not allow it to curdle. Now add the butter by degrees, until incorporated in the sauce. Season to taste with salt, add the fresh, chopped tarragon and parsley. Serves 4 to 6.

# Béchamel

1 *pint milk*
1½ *oz butter*
1½ *oz flour*

1 *half onion, finely sliced*
1 *bay leaf*
*salt and white pepper*

Gently simmer the onion and bay leaf in the milk for 10 minutes. Make a roux with the flour and butter, and add the strained milk by degrees, until you have a smooth sauce. Boil for 5 minutes or so, and taste for seasoning with salt and pepper.

# Bigarrade

½ *pint fonds lié*
*juice and zest of a Seville*
  *orange (or a sweet orange*

*plus the juice of half a*
  *lemon)*
*a glass of Burgundy*

Peel the orange clear of the pith. Cut zest into fine marmalade strips and plunge into boiling water for 2 minutes, then in cold water, strain. Put the *fonds lié* in a saucepan, add the juice of the orange and the glass of wine. Simmer for 5 minutes before adding the peel. Serves 4.

# Bread

¾ pint of milk
2½ oz butter
3 oz fresh white breadcrumbs
small onion

2 cloves
1 tablespoon cream
salt, pepper
bay leaf

Put the milk, butter, onion cut in half, cloves and bay leaf into a saucepan and bring to the boil. Allow to cook for a minute or two, remove from the heat, and leave for 20 minutes. Remove the onion, cloves and bay leaf, add the breadcrumbs, return to the heat, mashing the crumbs into the milk. Add the cream and adjust for seasoning. Serves 4–6.

# Champagne

This sauce is an English, Victorian recipe, probably unknown to the French. Mrs Bridges served it with baked ham. It is no more than a basic Espagnole or *fonds lié*, somewhat reduced and then thinned with champagne.

# Châteaubriand

Make exactly as you would a Béarnaise in the recipe on page 26, substituting white wine for vinegar. Before serving, add a scant teaspoonful of *glace de viande* or a tablespoonful of *demi-glace*, and finish with the butter, tarragon and parsley.

# Chaudfroid

A coating sauce, which can be brown or white. Many cooks make the white version by adding aspic to a Béchamel sauce, but Mrs Bridges correctly gives the recipe for a jellied Velouté, simply a roux to which jellied white stock is added, with cream as a liaison.

2 oz butter
3 oz flour
1 pint aspic, made with
    white veal stock

¼ pint of double cream
salt, white pepper

Make a roux with the butter and flour, and cook for a minute or two. Add the jelly and blend with the roux to a smooth sauce, cook for a further 5 minutes, and stir in the cream. Adjust the seasoning, and cook a further 5 minutes. Strain the sauce through a sieve or tammy.

For a brown Chaudfroid, use $\frac{3}{4}$ pint of *fonds lié*, to a half break-fastcupful of aspic, plus a $\frac{1}{4}$ ounce of gelatine powder. For the Quails in Aspic recipe on page 69, use any brown stock or game stock thickened with a brown roux, and add gelatine according to the amount of stock.

# Choron

This sauce is simply a Béarnaise, with the addition of a little tomato purée added for flavour and colour. It should be a delicate pink.

# Cumberland

| | |
|---|---|
| 4 *oranges* | 3 *tablespoons wine vinegar* |
| 2 *lemons* | $\frac{1}{4}$ *pint port wine* |
| 2 *teaspoons dry mustard* | 1 *lb redcurrant jelly* |
| 2 *shallots* | *salt and pepper* |

Peel the zest from the oranges and lemons clear of the pith, cut into marmalade strips and blanch by plunging into boiling water and boiling for 5 minutes. Drain and plunge into cold water. Squeeze the juice from two of the oranges and one lemon into a saucepan, add the rest of the ingredients, the marmalade strips. Boil, stirring until the jelly dissolves, then cook for a further 20 minutes. Allow to get cold before serving. Serves 6–8.

# Custard

In the 18th century, an Italian diplomat observed, 'In England there are sixty different religious groups, but only one sauce.' The sauce he was thinking of was melted butter, with which we smothered practically everything. Today, the sauces dominate the religions, and it is hard to decide which is *the* English sauce. The French think it is Mint Sauce, but the battle for supremacy lies between Tomato, Parsley and Custard, and perhaps above all, Custard is the most ubiquitous, and made with custard powder. Indeed, many people prefer Bird's Custard to that made with fresh eggs. Here is Mrs Bridges' recipe for the old-fashioned version.

| | |
|---|---|
| 2 *eggs* | ¾ *oz sugar* |
| ½ *pint milk* | *vanilla, pod or essence* |

Warm the milk in a double saucepan. Add the lightly beaten eggs and stir over a gentle heat. Add the sugar and the vanilla, and continue cooking until the mixture coats the back of the spoon. The custard should reach a point of thickness without curdling, but the more eggs you use, the thicker the sauce. Serves 3–4.

# Gooseberry

This is not intended to be a sweet sauce – it accompanies grilled mackerel – but the extreme tartness of green gooseberries needs the addition of a little sugar.

| | |
|---|---|
| ½ *lb green gooseberries* | ½ *pint milk* |
| 1 *oz butter* | 1 *tablespoon sugar* |
| 1 *tablespoon flour* | *salt, pepper, nutmeg* |

Stew the gooseberries until tender in a very little water. Press through a sieve to obtain a purée. Make a roux with the flour and butter, blend in the milk, add the sugar, a grating of nutmeg, salt and pepper. Cook for a minute or two, add the gooseberry purée, blend well and cook a further 5 minutes. If the sauce is too thick, add sufficient milk to thin it. Serves 4–6.

# Hollandaise

A similar preparation to the Béarnaise, a reduction of vinegar and herbs, with egg yolks and butter.

| | |
|---|---|
| 8 *tablespoons wine vinegar* | *blade of mace* |
| 2 *finely chopped shallots* | 6 *egg yolks* |
| 10 *peppercorns* | 5 *oz butter* |
| 1 *bay leaf* | *lemon juice* |

Reduce the wine vinegar with the herbs until you have two tablespoons of liquid. Beat egg yolks in a bowl, strain the vinegar into the eggs. Put the bowl in a pan of hot water, stir with a wooden spoon, increase the heat so the water begins to simmer, stir the sauce continuously. Add the butter bit by bit until all is incorporated with the sauce. Taste for seasoning, and add a squeeze of lemon. Hollandaise should be a smooth, creamy sauce with a slight tang. Serves 6–8.

# Horseradish

Mrs Bridges said that she always made the kitchen maids grate the horseradish root, 'otherwise my eyes are running all day and I can't cook if I can't see!' It is better to buy horseradish in the bottle, but if you are unfortunate enough to have some fresh root, here is the recipe:

3 tablespoons grated
   horseradish root
2 teaspoons wine vinegar

$\frac{1}{2}$ teaspoon dry mustard
$\frac{1}{4}$ pint thick cream
salt and white pepper

Horseradish can be grated with a blender, of course, or by hand. Mix the mustard with the vinegar in a bowl. Add the horseradish, salt and pepper and blend in the cream.

## Madère

Sauce Madère is simply a reduced Espagnole or *fonds lié*, returned to its previous consistency by the addition of Madeira wine.

## Mayonnaise

Mayonnaise can be soft and creamy, or as thick as butter and heavy with garlic, or it can come from a bottle, but the flavour of bottled mayonnaise is quite pronounced.
The ingredients should be at room temperature. Put an egg yolk into a bowl and add, extremely slowly, a thin trickle of olive oil while stirring the yolk. As the sauce begins to thicken you can be more generous with the oil. To make it really solid, use two yolks, and plenty of oil. Season with salt and white pepper to taste, and add a teaspoon of white wine vinegar to counteract the blandness, and to thin the mayonnaise if needed.

# Mornay

A cheese Béchamel, adding either grated Gruyère cheese or Parmesan cheese to the Béchamel recipe, the cheese in quantities to suit the dish which it accompanies.

# Mustard

1 *oz butter*
½ *oz flour*
1 *breakfastcup milk*
2 *teaspoons dry mustard*

1 *teaspoon white wine vinegar*
*salt and pepper*
3 *tablespoons thick cream*

Melt butter in a saucepan, add the flour and the mustard. Add the milk gradually, blending until smooth. Add vinegar, salt and pepper, and cook for 5 minutes, stirring now and then. Add cream, and taste the sauce for seasoning and piquancy. Add more mustard if required. Serves 4.

# Parsley

The secret, according to Mrs Bridges, is 'plenty of finely chopped parsley. The sauce should not be white, with green specks in it, as one so often sees, but thick, green and creamy.'

*Béchamel Sauce*
*a large handful of parsley*

*butter*
*salt and pepper*

Chop the parsley, washed free of grit, very finely, preferably with a Mouli parsley mill. Add by degrees to the hot Béchamel, and incorporate a nut of butter. Adjust for seasoning, and serve.

# Périgueux

Périgueux is a fine, classic sauce based on the Espagnole. Use either Espagnole or *fonds lié*, reduce, then return to previous consistency with Madeira wine. Add truffle essence and finely chopped truffles. When the truffles are cut into tiny rounds, and *foie gras* purée is blended into the sauce, it becomes a Sauce Périgourdine.

# Port Wine

1 *large glass Port wine*
2 *minced shallots*
*sprig of thyme*

1 *orange*, 1 *lemon*
$\frac{1}{2}$ *pint fonds lié*
*salt and cayenne pepper*

Put the shallots, thyme and Port into a saucepan. Boil, and reduce to half the quantity. Peel the zest free of the pith of the orange and lemon, and cut into marmalade strips. Blanch, by plunging the strips into boiling water, boil 5 minutes, then plunge into cold water, strain. Remove the thyme from the Port, add the strips of zest, the juice of the fruit, the *fonds lié*, and bring to the boil. Skim if needed, taste for seasoning. Serves 4–6.

# Zingara

Should be prepared with fresh tomatoes and not purée.

$\frac{1}{2}$ *pint fonds lié*
6 *tomatoes*

*truffle essence*
2 *slices cooked ham*

Slice the tomatoes, and stew them in a little butter until they are soft. They can be stewed for 30 minutes – the longer the better – over a gentle heat in a covered saucepan. Press them through a sieve to obtain a purée. Bring the *fonds lié* to simmering point, add the finely diced ham and truffle essence. Cook for 5 minutes, add the tomato purée, and cook a further 10 minutes. Taste for seasoning. If the sauce is a little sharp, add a small amount of caster sugar until the flavour is adjusted – the sharpness will be due to the tomatoes. Serves 4–6.

# SOUPS

Mrs Bridges' original cookery book gave recipes for forty soups, 'only half of my repertoire'. During her training she had to learn at least eighty soups, to suit all occasions and seasons. Soups were popular because they were filling and because Edwardian cooks were expected to be economical and thrifty. Nothing was wasted, and most scraps found their way into the stockpot. Even so, cooks were aware that really good soups can only be made with good, fresh ingredients, especially those to be sent 'upstairs'. Yet the food enjoyed by the servants was often equally enjoyed in the dining-room. 'Easy to turn a plain dish into a fancy one,' comments Mrs Bridges, tongue-in-cheek, 'the servants like my potato soup, and when I've added a little cream and a handful of croûtons, it goes upstairs as Potage Parmentier.' From the kitchen came the best of both worlds.

Soups of the early 1900s included Palestine Soup, so called because it was made with Jerusalem artichokes; Portable Soup, which you reduced to a jelly or marmite, and stored in jars; and the famous Turtle Soup enjoyed only by the privileged few, and, traditionally, at the Lord Mayor's Banquet. Mrs Beeton gives a long and complicated recipe for grappling with a turtle and turning it into soup. Mrs Bridges preferred short cuts. 'Turtle soup,' she wrote, 'is best purchased in tins. Just add a glass of sherry before serving.' At the turn of the century, tinned soups were readily available and many found their way 'upstairs', disguised, perhaps, by the addition of a little brown roux, a teaspoon of Bovril, a glass of wine. Mrs Bridges had very decided views on all aspects of cooking, and soup making was no exception. We have chosen twelve of the most popular recipes from her collection, including the ubiquitous Brown Windsor Soup – a 'downstairs' favourite – the elegant Tortue Claire and Crème Princesse for special occasions.

Of the golden rules of soup making, Mrs Bridges wrote: 'Clean out your stockpot every day, and always leave stock in an enamelled pan. Stock which contains both meat and vegetables should be boiled at least once a day, otherwise it is inclined to sour, but it will keep longer if a cauliflower is one of the vegetables used. When you make a clear stock, never allow it to boil. It should simmer slowly for at least four hours, and be well skimmed, especially during the preliminary simmering. Any vegetables added must be thoroughly clean, the meat as lean as possible. Be very careful when you season your stock or soup. An oversalted consommé might as well be thrown away, while salty thick soups and broths can be corrected by adding one or two potatoes and a little sugar. Most soups are best made the day before they are needed, and preparation in advance saves time and temper. An hour lost in the morning has to be run after all day.'

We can make soups in a fraction of the time it took Mrs Bridges. She had to force everything through a fine sieve, having first pounded ingredients in a mortar, for there were no quick food mills or blenders. Today's soups are smoother and creamier and, if anything, more economical. Mrs Bridges would have approved.

# SOUPS

## The Upstairs Recipes

Consommé de
  Volaille
Crème St Germain
Crème Princesse
Velouté à la Reine
Tortue Claire
Game Soup

Many classic soups can be made from the following basic consommé recipe, with the addition of a few ingredients. We have selected some delicious recipes, in which frozen or tinned ingredients may be utilised, saving time although they may be marginally more expensive in certain instances.

# Consommé de Volaille

(Prepare the day before needed)

1 *lb lean beef, preferably shin*
   *beef bones*
4–5 *lb boiling chicken*
5 *pints water*
2 *teaspoonsful of salt*

*an onion, carrot, turnip*
1 *stick of celery*
*thyme and 2 bay leaves*
6 *peppercorns*

Roast the chicken for 30 minutes at 425°, until lightly browned. Place in a large 12-pint stewpan with the beef and the bones. Cover with water and bring to simmering point (about 20 minutes) removing scum as it rises. Continue to remove scum until the stock is clear, and don't allow it to boil. Now add the vegetables, peeled and sliced, the herbs, salt and peppercorns. Cook for 4 hours. Strain stock into a bowl and leave overnight. Remove fat from the surface and transfer the stock to a clean pan, watching for the sediment at the bottom. Beat two egg whites and whisk into the stock; put the pan on the heat. Whisk while it comes to the boil, and as the foam begins to rise, remove from the heat, allowing it to subside. Repeat this once more, but without whisking. Strain through a clean cloth into a bowl. The stock should now be clear and bright. If it is still cloudy, wait until it has become cold before repeating the process.

# Chicken Purée

Remove the meat from the chicken, reserving the breasts. Pass through a food mill, such as a Mouli, then through a fine sieve, or use an electric blender. Add stock to the consistency of a thick cream. The meat from the breasts is used as a garnish.

# Crème St Germain

2 pints chicken consommé
1 lb large peas (frozen ones
   will do very well)
a few spring onions, or one
   small onion
a small lettuce

mint
1 oz flour
1 oz butter
4 oz petit pois
$\frac{1}{4}$ pint thick cream
salt, cayenne pepper

Finely shred the lettuce and slice the onions. Add the peas.
Simmer in the stock until tender, with the mint.
Pass through a food mill, then through a sieve, or use a blender.
Make a roux with butter and flour, and add the pea purée gradually. Bring to the boil, add the petit pois and cook for 5 minutes.
Add the cream and correct the seasoning – the soup may taste
too sweet, so add a little more salt and a dash of cayenne pepper
to taste. If the petit pois are fresh, cook them until tender in a
little salted water before adding to the soup. Serves 4.

# Crème Princesse

1 lb asparagus
2 pints consommé
1 pint chicken purée
1 oz each of flour and butter

$\frac{1}{4}$ pint cream
diced chicken garnish
chervil

Cut heads off the asparagus. Simmer the stalks until tender in the
consommé. If frozen asparagus is used, this will take about 10
minutes. Pass through Mouli, sieve, or purée in blender. Now
make a roux with the butter and flour. Add the asparagus purée
and the consommé in which it has cooked. Add the chicken
purée and boil gently for 5 minutes. If the Crème is not smooth,
you will need to pass it through the sieve once more. Correct the
seasoning, add the cream. Cook the asparagus tips in salted
water until tender, drain, and add to the Crème, also the diced
chicken and chopped chervil. Serves 4.

# Velouté à la Reine

2 pints chicken consommé
$\frac{3}{4}$ pint chicken purée
2 tablespoonsful ground rice
3 egg yolks

$\frac{1}{4}$ pint cream
1 oz butter
diced chicken garnish

Mix rice to a paste with water or stock. Add chicken purée to the consommé, then add the rice paste. Boil gently for 10 minutes. Beat eggs with the cream. Remove the soup from the heat, stir in the egg and cream mixture. Add butter, stir and correct for seasoning. Add garnish of diced chicken before serving. Serves 4.

## Tortue Claire

To every 2 pints of chicken consommé, add a tin of real turtle soup. Make an infusion of herbs, soaking either fresh or dried herbs in a little boiling water until they have imparted their flavour. The herbs, called 'Turtle herbs' are as follows: coriander, peppercorns, thyme, marjoram, basil, rosemary, sage, bay leaves. Add the infusion to the soup. Thicken with two teaspoonsful of arrowroot, and add a large glass of Madeira or dry sherry before serving. Serves 6.

## Game Soup

3 *pints chicken stock*
*pheasant, partridge or*
  *grouse carcasses*
*an onion stuck with two*
  *or three cloves*
*small piece of garlic*
2 *sliced carrots*

*bouquet garni*
*a large glass red wine*
1 *oz flour*
1 *oz butter*
*sherry*
*salt and cayenne*

Simmer the carcasses in the stock with the vegetables, herbs and wine. Skim when necessary, and allow to simmer for about 3 hours. Strain, and remove all the meat left on the carcasses. Pass through a food mill, and add the meat purée to the soup. Make a roux with the flour and butter and gradually add it to the soup to thicken. Simmer for 10 minutes. Add salt and cayenne to taste. Add sherry just before serving, and, if liked, a few croûtons. Serves 4.

# SOUPS

## The Downstairs Recipes

Brown Windsor
Mulligatawny
Oxtail
Pea and Ham
Potato and Leek

# Brown Windsor Soup

2 lb shin beef
beef bones
2 oz barley, soaked overnight
a large onion and two carrots
3–4 sticks celery
2 leeks

2 oz butter
2 oz flour
4 pints water
bouquet garni
1 bay leaf
1 wine glass Madeira

Roast the meat and the bones in the oven at 425° for about 40 minutes, or until browned. Meanwhile, flour the vegetables, which should be sliced, and fry them in the butter until browned. Add the roasted meat, the water, the bouquet garni and the barley. Bring to a simmering point and skim whenever necessary. Allow the soup to cook for at least 4 hours in a part-covered pan. Strain, and pass the meat and vegetables through a sieve. Season with salt and black pepper before reheating. Add the Madeira before serving. Serves 6.


# Mulligatawny Soup

4 pints good chicken stock
4 onions
6 tomatoes
1 cupful fresh coconut milk
    or an infusion from
    desiccated coconut
2 bay leaves
a cinnamon stick

small piece fresh ginger root
1 dessertspoonful each of
    coriander seeds, cumin
    seeds, powdered turmeric
a half teaspoonful of chilli
    powder
6 peppercorns
salt to taste

This soup seems to have been a great favourite with the men of the household, both upstairs and downstairs. 'An Indian soup,' writes Mrs Bridges, 'which I don't much care for myself, and everyone seems to have a different recipe. I'm sure mine is correct.'

Like kedgeree, mulligatawny soup passed via the Anglo-Indians into the British Army, and thence 'home'. Chicken or lamb would have been the meat ingredient, and rice was usually added to make the soup go further.

The spices must first be well pounded, and lightly roasted for about 5 minutes. Fry them in an ounce of butter, then add the coconut milk and the stock, the bay leaves, the cinnamon and the ginger. Add the tomatoes, and two of the onions, finely sliced. Gently simmer for 30 minutes in a covered pan. Strain,

and pass the vegetables through a sieve. Slice the remaining onions finely, and fry them in butter until lightly brown. Add these to the soup and, if wished, a cupful of boiled rice. This soup bears little resemblance to the commercial product available in tins, which is dark brown and thick, and which in turn bears little resemblance to the original. Serves 8–10.

## Oxtail Soup

an oxtail, cut into pieces
2 oz flour
3 onions
a carrot, a turnip and
  a stick of celery

parsley, thyme
4 pints water
salt and pepper

Slice the onions, carrot, turnip and celery. Fry them in good beef dripping, or in oil for 5 minutes. Add the oxtail, and sprinkle meat and vegetables with the flour. Fry for a further 10–15 minutes, turning the meat and allowing it to lightly brown. Add the water and the herbs, the salt and pepper and allow to simmer for 3 hours, skimming when necessary. Remove the oxtail pieces, strain the soup, pass the vegetables through a sieve, and add the meat from the tail bones. Taste and season if required. This soup should be made well in advance and allowed to get completely cold, when excess fat can be removed. Serves 8–10.

## Pea and Ham Soup

cooked ham-bone and the
  remains of its meat
1 lb split green peas, soaked
  overnight
an onion, stuck with two or
  three cloves

a heaped teaspoonful sugar
2 potatoes
3 pints water
salt and pepper

Make this soup after you have served a ham, and there is a ham-bone and enough meat left to flavour the soup. Put all the ingredients in a large pan, and let them simmer until the peas are tender (about 1–1½ hours). Remove the ham-bone, and pass the soup through a fine sieve. Add any shredded meat that remains before serving. Taste for seasoning. Serves 6–8.

# Potato and Leek Soup

2 *lb potatoes*
4 *medium size leeks*
1 *oz butter*
*yolks of two eggs*

1 *pint milk*
1 *pint water*
*salt and white pepper*

Finely slice the white parts of the leeks, and sauté them in the butter. Peel and quarter the potatoes, and add them to the leeks. Add the milk and water and cook until the potatoes are soft. Pass the vegetables through a sieve. Lightly beat the yolks of the eggs, add them to the soup and allow to thicken, but take great care not to let the soup boil, otherwise it will curdle. Additional potatoes make the soup thicker, the eggs make it richer. Serves 4–6.

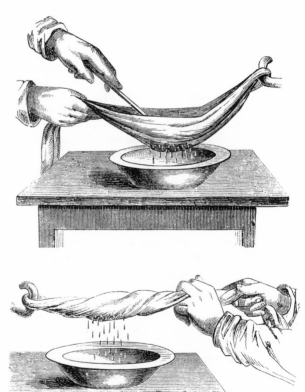

# FISH

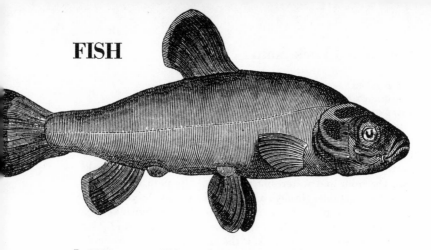

In 1903, you could buy a lobster for a shilling, and scallops were
9d a dozen – scallops today can cost thirty new pence each.
According to Mrs Bridges, the fishmonger arrived before seven
in the morning on Fridays. He brought fresh fish, packed in ice,
straight from Billingsgate in a van (horse-drawn of course) to
Eaton Place. As there was no domestic refrigeration, Fridays
and Saturdays were fish days. On other days of the week, the
fishmonger sold poultry, eggs and game, as fishmongers still do.
Turbot was very popular, because a fair-size fish would feed an
entire household, and many cooks had a special turbot-kettle in
which to poach it. Bloaters, too, were a favourite, and whitebait
from the Thames, even though 'they make the whole house smell'.
Cod was 'at its best around Christmas time', and John Dory,
which seems to have gone out of fashion, was 'a great favourite,
baked in a paper case'. Mrs Bridges included a chapter on freshwater fish, which had been in plentiful supply during her years
of training at Southwold. The Estate provided the cooks with
trout and pike and tench. 'Some people,' sniffs Mrs Bridges,
'think that what costs nothing is good for nothing, but then they
never tasted my stuffed pike, or my water souchy.' 'Water
souchy' had somehow found its way into the Victorian repertoire from the Flemish *Waterzoi*, a fish stew. It was simply a dish
of stewed, assorted fish, served with parsley. Curiously though,
Mrs Bridges omits a recipe for *quenelles* of pike, which she would
certainly have learned to make under Mrs Harcourt, who
had trained at the Carlton Hotel. The French dishes which we
have chosen from Mrs Bridges' book are Lobster Bouchées, a
nice dish for a summer day; and Sole Belgravia, a rather grand
dish of sole invented by Mrs B, and glazed with two sauces
of different colours, which makes an impressive presentation.

In the 'downstairs' section there's Eel Pie, Cod with Parsley Sauce, which sometimes went upstairs, the cod glazed with Oyster Sauce and dressed with oysters and fried parsley; Baked Grey Mullet, which some cooks considered an inferior fish, an opinion not shared by Mrs Bridges who wrote, 'an inferior cook cannot help but produce an inferior dish'. Of the various points to watch in fish cookery, Mrs Bridges says, 'Don't wash your fish too much, or they may lose their flavour. Take care not to disturb the scales of freshwater fish, and soak them in salt water for at least two hours before cooking. A little salt and vinegar put into the water when boiling fish makes the flesh firm. Always drain boiled fish very carefully before serving [in Mrs Bridges' day, boiled fish was often served on a white napkin] and if you cover it with a sauce, make the sauce extra thick, so that it will blend with residual water from the fish. When poaching a salmon, add a pinch of bicarbonate of soda to the water – it preserves the colour of the fish. To remove the odour of fish from pans, always wash with soda, then rub a piece of butter around the inside of the pan. Another method is to clean the pan with vinegar, then wash in the ordinary way.'

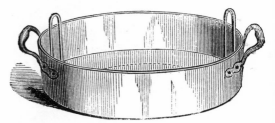

# FISH

## The Upstairs Recipes

Mrs Bridges' Fish Pie
Sole Belgravia
Lobster Bouchées
Baked Stuffed Pike
Kedgeree
Whitebait

# Fish Pie

2 lb white fish (hake,
  haddock or cod)
two whiting
4 oz peeled prawns
lobster tails
¼ lb mushrooms
a large leek or two
  medium-sized ones

¼ lb butter
anchovy essence
a few peeled grapes
1 tablespoonful cream
2 oz plain flour
¾ pint milk
1½ lb potatoes
salt, pepper, paprika, fennel

Put the whiting in a pint of water, bring to the boil, and simmer gently for 40 minutes, breaking the fish up with a fork during cooking. Strain liquid into another pan, and reduce until you have a mere half cupful of concentrated stock. While this is reducing, poach the white fish in milk until tender. Make a roux with 2 oz flour and 2 oz butter, and gently add the milk in which the fish has cooked, until of a consistency which coats the back of the spoon. Add the fish concentrate, a little anchovy essence, a few grains of fennel seed, salt, pepper and a good teaspoonful of paprika. Finely slice the leek and the mushrooms, and cook them gently in butter. Peel and boil the potatoes. Mix the cooked white fish with prawns, lobster tails, leek and mushrooms, the peeled grapes, the sauce enriched with a tablespoonful of cream. Place all in a fireproof pie dish. Mash potatoes with milk and butter, season with salt and white pepper. Cover the pie dish, dot with small pieces of butter, and cook in a moderate oven, 350° for 30 minutes, or until the top is nicely browned. Serves 4.

# Sole Belgravia

4 soles
5 whiting
1½ oz flour

1 oz butter
¼ pint milk
1 egg

Skin the sole, leaving the head and tail intact. Remove the backbone by lifting the fillets with a sharp, pointed knife, cutting almost to the edge of the fish, removing the backbone with kitchen scissors. Boil the whiting with the bones for 30 minutes, strain the stock into a bowl. Place the stock back on the heat, and boil to reduce half the quantity. Pick as much meat as possible from the whiting and mince or pound it very fine. This

forcemeat is to be mixed with a roux of flour, butter and milk. Boil a $\frac{1}{4}$ pint of milk with 1 oz butter, then add 1 oz flour. Beat off the fire, until the paste is smooth, and leaves the sides of the pan. Cool, and mix with the fish forcemeat and a beaten egg. Stuff the soles with this mixture and poach them, stuffing side down (it helps the stuffing to remain intact) until tender, in a *bain-marie* at about 325°. Meanwhile make the sauce:

Take a large wineglassful of white wine, add 4 peppercorns, and a bouquet garni, also one finely chopped shallot. Boil until reduced to about a tablespoonful. Meanwhile, make a roux with 1 oz butter and 1 oz flour. Add fish stock gradually, until well blended and free from lumps. Strain the wine, add it to the sauce. Cook for 10 minutes, add a good tablespoonful of thick cream. Very carefully, transfer the poached sole onto a serving dish, draining any liquid from the fish. Mask one half of each sole, along its length, with a little of the white sauce. Add to the remaining sauce a heaped teaspoonful of tomato purée, mix well, and mask the other half of each fish with the pink sauce.

NB. It is important not to over-sauce. Serves 4.


# Lobster Bouchées

This recipe uses cooked lobster. The Victorians were fond of 'Lobster Patties', which was lobster in a Béchamel sauce cooked in little pastry cases – *vol-au-vents* and *bouchées*, in other words.

| | |
|---|---|
| 10 *oz puff pastry* | $\frac{1}{4}$ *lb button mushrooms* |
| *cooked lobster* | *fennel seeds* |
| *Mornay sauce* | *salt and cayenne pepper* |

Roll out the pastry to a thickness of $\frac{1}{4}$-inch. Brush the surface with beaten egg. With a pastry cutter of $2\frac{1}{2}$-inches diameter, cut circles, and lift each on to a baking sheet. With a knife, or a cutter of $1\frac{1}{2}$ inches, mark circles on each of the rounds of pastry, taking care to centre them. Bake in a hot oven, 425°, until well risen and lightly browned. Cool, and remove the centre circles, scooping any moist pastry that remains in the cases – the small circles are the lids of the *bouchées*.

Prepare the filling as follows. Make a sauce Mornay, add the peeled, button mushrooms, a sprinkling of fennel seeds or powdered fennel – but take care, for fennel has a powerful flavour. Season to taste with salt and cayenne pepper, and lastly add the lobster meat, cut into small pieces or cubes. Stir into the sauce, and allow the whole to become thoroughly hot. Spoon the mixture into the cases, placing a lid on each; fill the cases quite generously, return them to the oven at 350° for 5 minutes, and serve. Serves 6.

## Baked Stuffed Pike

a 3–4 lb pike, gutted and
   scaled but with head and
   tail intact
a medium-sized onion
1½ oz fresh white
   breadcrumbs
parsley

lemon rind
2 anchovy fillets
milk
¼ bottle red wine mixed
   with juice of two oranges
dried sage, salt and pepper
wedges of lemon

Slice and mince the onion finely, and cook until soft in butter. Put the onion in a bowl with the breadcrumbs, finely chopped parsley, chopped anchovy fillets, grated lemon rind, crumbled sage, salt and pepper. Add sufficient milk to make a stiff filling. Fill the cavity of the fish with this mixture, and sew with thread, cobbling or lacing, as one laces shoes. Spread some butter evenly over the pike, and place it in a baking dish with the wine and orange juice. Shake some salt over the fish, and a little black pepper. Bake in an oven at 350°, basting occasionally. The fish will take about 25 minutes. Test with a skewer to see whether the flesh is firm, remove from the oven and serve. Wedges of lemon and plenty of parsley should accompany this dish. Serves 4–6.

## Kedgeree

'Kedgeree', says Mrs Bridges, 'is a man's dish', perhaps because it was brought over from India with the British Army, where it was known as *Khichari*, and the native version recognises it as a vegetarian dish of lentils, rice, onions and curried eggs. Back 'home' where it featured as an offering at the masculine breakfast, cooks added smoked haddock, or sometimes salt cod. It stood on the sideboard, next to the kidneys and bacon; this was the breakfast of yesteryear – who eats it today? 'Serve a good breakfast,' pronounced Mrs Bridges, 'and the rest of the day's dishes will be better received.'

| 1 lb smoked haddock | salt and pepper |
| 6 oz Patna or Basmatti rice | curry spices: coriander, |
| 2 oz butter | cumin, turmeric, ginger, |
| 4 hard-boiled eggs | cinnamon, chilli – or curry |
| chopped parsley | powder |

Put the rice in a saucepan with a close-fitting lid. Add 1½ breakfastcupfuls of cold water and a teaspoonful of salt. Cook over a very low flame for 15 minutes, or until the rice is tender. Meanwhile, poach the haddock in water, and pass the hard-boiled eggs through a sieve. The curry spices must be well pounded and blended, and in the proportion of a level dessert-spoonful for the above amount of rice. Alternatively, use commercial curry powder. Cook the curry spices in the butter for 3 minutes, then add the drained, cooked rice and the fish, broken up with a fork. Add half the sieved eggs, and gently blend all together, turning over with the fork. Taste for seasoning. Cook until the kedgeree is nicely hot, and serve on a silver breakfast dish, sprinkling the remaining egg as a decoration. Serves 4–6.

# Whitebait

Although Mrs Bridges declared that whitebait were 'a nuisance, and very bothersome', they were a very popular dish of the day. Possibly she was referring to the cooking smells, shared with bloaters and sprats, which were said to 'pervade every corner of the house'. During the 19th century, whitebait swarmed up the Thames beyond Greenwich, and were of consequence readily available. (Fresh whitebait and frozen whitebait are simply not the same thing at all.) Of their cooking, Mrs Bridges has this to say:

'On no account should whitebait be floured in advance. They must be lightly tossed in fine flour, and instantly fried in deep, *smoking* fat for as long as it takes to walk round the kitchen table. Have the serving dish by your side, with plenty of lemon wedges, parsley and thinly sliced brown bread and butter. The butler or housemaid must take them to the table without delay. They should, in fact, run with them. This is the only proper way to prepare and serve whitebait.'

And how long did Mrs B take to walk around her kitchen table? Six seconds? Anyway, as soon as the fish are curled and crisply brown, transfer them to the serving dish, and run if you like.

# FISH

## The Downstairs Recipes

Baked Grey Mullet
Cod with Parsley
   Sauce
Eel Pie
Grilled or Poached
   Mackerel with
   Gooseberry Sauce
Jellied Eels

# Baked Grey Mullet

Only recently has the true quality of this fish been appreciated, and mainly by the French, who grill it with fennel, or bake it with tomatoes. Mrs Bridges seems to have anticipated the French method, for she included baked mullet, with tomatoes but minus the garlic. . . .

4 mullet, cleaned and scaled,
   keeping the heads and tails
   on
1½ lb tomatoes peeled and chopped
a dozen shallots finely sliced

parsley
capers
lemon juice and thyme
mustard, salt, pepper

Make diagonal incisions along each side of the fish, about three per side. In these incisions force some butter. Salt and pepper the mullet, and put them in a greased baking dish. Put the shallots, tomatoes, the chopped parsley, thyme, capers, a teaspoonful of dry mustard in a saucepan, and simmer for 15 minutes, or until there has been a reduction, and the sauce thickens. Pour this into the baking dish with the fish, and bake in a moderate oven, 350° until the mullet are tender, about 25 minutes. Transfer to a serving dish, pour the sauce over the fish, then sprinkle them with the lemon juice and serve. Serves 4.

# Cod with Parsley Sauce

The cod, either in steaks or fillets, or even as a whole fish (when you would require a sizeable fish kettle) should be gently poached in a *court bouillon*: water to cover, about ½ cup of vinegar, a few black peppercorns, ½ teaspoon of fennel seeds. Cook until tender, lift out and drain carefully. With a sharp knife, remove the skin. Cooks used to serve poached or boiled cod on a crisp, white napkin, so as to absorb any residual liquor from the cooking.

Decorate with a sprinkling of capers and chopped parsley, and serve with boiled potatoes and lashings of Parsley Sauce (see page 31).

# Eel Pie

3 *eels*
3 *hard-boiled eggs*
2 *shallots*
½ *oz butter*
2 *glasses dry sherry*
2 *oz flour*

2 *oz butter*
*juice of a lemon*
8 *oz puff pastry*
*parsley, nutmeg, cayenne*
   *pepper, salt*

Gently stew the eels in water to cover. When they are cooked, skin and bone them, reserving the cooking liquor. Chop the shallots and cook them in the butter for 5 minutes, add the sherry, a good bunch of finely chopped parsley, a little grated nutmeg, salt and cayenne to taste. Add the pieces of eel to this mixture, and simmer gently. Meanwhile, make a roux with the flour and butter, add the strained fish stock gradually, blending until smooth. Add lemon juice. Put the eels and shallot mixture into a pie dish, of a size sufficient to contain them, add quarters of hard-boiled eggs, then the white sauce. Cover the pie dish with puff pastry and bake at 425° for 12 minutes, then turn oven down to 325°, and cook a further 20 minutes. Serves 4–6.

# Grilled or Poached
# Mackerel with Gooseberry Sauce

Small mackerel are best grilled or fried. They have more flavour than large ones, which should be poached. Cut off the head, trim the fins and tail, and make three or four diagonal incisions each side of the fish, pressing a nut of butter mixed with chopped tarragon into the cuts. Salt well, and cook under a hot grill or over charcoal.

For poached mackerel, fillet the fish, and poach in a *court bouillon* as follows:

Equal parts of water and white wine to cover the fish, add a sliced onion, two bay leaves, a few peppercorns, a sliced carrot, a stalk of celery cut into small pieces, a sprig of thyme and parsley, salt. Simmer gently for 30 minutes before adding the fish, replacing with more liquid if it reduces. Poach the mackerel until tender – about 12 minutes. Serve grilled or poached mackerel with Gooseberry Sauce (see page 29).

# Jellied Eels

3 *lb eels*
5 *teaspoonsful salt*
1 *pint water*
3 *tablespoons malt vinegar*

1 *onion*
*bay leaves and peppercorns*
*parsley*
*lemon juice*

Chop the eels into 2-inch pieces and plunge them into boiling water with the salt. Take off the boil, and let them stand for 5 minutes. Put the eels in a large stewpan, add the pint of water – or sufficient to cover—vinegar, sliced onion, a few bay leaves, parsley, lemon juice, more salt, peppercorns. Bring to the boil, reduce and simmer for 20 minutes, by which time the eels should be tender.

Remove the pieces of eel to a serving dish, deep enough to contain the liquid. Strain the liquid over the eels, and when cool, refrigerate for several hours. The quantity of eels to the pint of water should be sufficient to jellify – the parsley gives the jelly the traditional hint of green, like the sea. The jelly should be soft, not too set. However, if it fails, it might be necessary to add a little gelatine, but not too much, otherwise the jelly will be stiff. Serves 6–8.

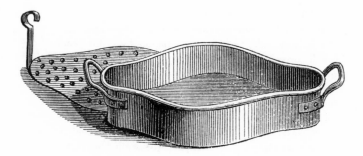

# GAME AND POULTRY

'Would pheasant be so esteemed by the gentry if it were available the year round, and by one and all if it were cheap and in plentiful supply?' asks Mrs Bridges in a philosophical frame of mind, and adds, 'like whelks and winkles?' More than seventy years later the season is still strictly prescribed; pheasant may only be stalked over a field of snow, or across a carpet of copper-hued leaves, even though most fruits and vegetables have broken their bounds. Strawberries in January? Mrs Bridges would have had none of it.

During the winter months there was an abundance of game at Eaton Place, because Lady Marjorie Bellamy's father had an estate at Southwold, and one in Scotland, near Blair Castle in Perthshire, where Hudson the butler's father was head ghillie. Mrs Bridges writes, 'There is always plenty of venison through the winter, which I send up in collops, in stews, roasted with whinberry sauce, or in Game Pie. We have grouse, which the gentry likes plain cooked, or later in the season we have them stoved.'

The first of the season's game reached Eaton Place in mid-August. The young grouse were an eagerly awaited event – 'up to our knees in feathers'. In the kitchen of Eaton Place, Mrs Bridges would have been the only person who knew how to pluck and dress poultry; it requires skill and long practice. Grouse are in season from August 12th until December 10th, and are at their best during late August and October. 'Grouse,' writes Mrs Bridges, 'should hang from three days to a fortnight, and only the young birds should be roasted. Old grouse are best braised, or "stoved" as the Scots say – they used to send them down from Blair with a label attached to the leg marked with an

"S" if the birds were old. Roast grouse should always be served with game chips, bread sauce, redcurrant or rowan jelly, and a bunch of watercress.

'We get the grouse and venison from Scotland, and sometimes ptarmigan. Harris [the head keeper at Southwold] sends up pheasant and partridge and hare. Thank goodness it is pouched before it arrives here. Most of the game is well nigh hung and ready to cook before it gets to London; we never have to hang it long. Some gentlemen are very fond of Hare Pie, some prefer it jugged; and some of the London servants won't touch hare, declaring it to be vermin.'

At the turn of the century, species of birds declared as 'game' included ortolans, larks, corncrakes, thrushes and warblers, now protected by ornithologists, but still devoutly pursued on the continent of Europe. It is doubtful whether larks or thrushes ever featured on the menus of Eaton Place, for Mrs Bridges does not mention them, and she was no ornithologist. 'Ptarmigan,' she claims, 'is otherwise called Norwegian Grouse, and is the same bird as the Red Grouse, but whose plumage has been affected by climate. Ptarmigan often taste of turpentine, they being very fond of pine cones. They have no value to the cook.'

For the majority of the population, poultry was quite as rare as game, chicken being a special treat on certain Sundays of the year, while goose and turkey were never seen either side of Christmas; chicken was usually boiled, for boiling fowls were cheaper and larger than roasters. The wealthier classes, however, enjoyed chicken prepared in a variety of ways, most of them from the French repertoire. Mrs Bridges gives several recipes for chicken, and we have chosen her Poulet Sauté Demidov, cooked with vegetables and truffles; and the more humble but none the less delicious chicken pie. 'Chicken Asquith' seems to have been an invention of Mrs Bridges, probably on the occasion of Herbert Asquith's visit to Eaton Place. The dish has an interesting history. Mrs Bridges says that she learned to stuff a chicken with rosemary and juniper berries which her mother, in turn, had been shown by Northamptonshire gypsies – it certainly isn't a traditional English recipe. 'Chicken Asquith' is pot-roasted, and a sauce of game stock, the juniper-flavoured juices from the chicken, swilled with Madeira, is then thickened with a roux and finished with cream, a delicious way of preparing chicken. Equally delicious is the recipe for Pheasant with mandarin oranges – *Faisan Suc de Mandarine*; Wild Duck with Port Wine from Southwold where, it seems, there was always plenty of both, and Mrs Bridges' famous Quails in Aspic.

# GAME AND POULTRY

## The Upstairs Recipes

Chicken Asquith
Poulet Sauté
   Demidov
Pheasant Mandarin
Quails in Aspic
Caneton Sauvage
   au Porto
Game Pie
Roast Grouse
Braised Grouse
Roast Partridge
Partridge Pie
Partridge Pudding
Jugged Hare
Venison

# Chicken Asquith

a 3–4 lb roasting chicken
2 oz butter
½ pint game or chicken stock
a dozen juniper berries
fresh rosemary

1 oz butter
1 oz flour
1 wine glass Madeira or sherry
cream
salt, cayenne pepper

Put the crushed juniper berries and a good sprig of rosemary inside the chicken. Coat generously with butter, and season with salt. Put the chicken in a covered casserole or earthenware 'brick' for an hour at 350°, or until tender. Remove the chicken from the pot, take out the rosemary and discard it. Scrape the juniper berries from inside the carcass, and mix them with the juices that remain in the casserole. Turn the oven temperature up to 400–425°. Swill the juices with the Madeira. Put the chicken on a baking dish, and return it to the oven in order to brown it. Put the game stock and the Madeira/juniper-flavoured stock in a pan over a high heat, and boil until reduced by half. Make a roux with the butter and the flour, and add the reduced, strained stock by degrees, until you have a smooth, thick sauce. Add salt and cayenne pepper to taste. Add a good tablespoonful of thick cream to the sauce, and pour over the browned chicken. Serve at once. Serves 4.


# Poulet Sauté Demidov

This was apparently a very popular dish at Eaton Place, usually served to distinguished guests. It belongs to the standard repertoire of French cuisine, and it isn't difficult to make, apart from the careful preparation of vegetables.

a 3–4 lb roasting chicken
2 medium-sized carrots
1 turnip
2 stalks of celery
a dozen tiny onions

¼ lb small mushrooms
8 oz puff pastry
a wine glass of Madeira
a truffle
Espagnole sauce or demi-glace

Prepare the vegetables in advance, as follows: peel the turnip and onions, scrape the carrots. The turnip and carrots should be sliced about ¼-inch thick, and cut into ribbed or fluted crescents. While this is not essential, and of course makes no difference to the *taste* of the dish, it is the appearance that matters. 'A cook who serves up a dish that looks like an unmade bed,' writes Mrs Bridges with a rare attempt at humour, 'has no business being in service.' The mushrooms should be cut into fluted spirals, using a sharp pointed knife, or a vegetable cutter. Take half the prepared carrots, turnip and also the onions, and sauté them in butter for 10 minutes. Joint the chicken, seal in butter until lightly browned. Place in a sauté dish, a cocotte or casserole with the sautéed vegetables. Cover and cook for 45 minutes in an oven set at 350°. Meanwhile, sauté the rest of the vegetables in butter until they are tender, also the mushrooms. This cooking of the other half of the vegetables ensures that they retain their shape, and can be used as a garnish. Those with the chicken are more likely to break up during the oven cooking.

Roll out the puff pastry, cut into fluted crescents with a pastry cutter and bake at 425° until well risen and brown, but take care not to overcook them, as they burn quickly. Remove the chicken from the cocotte, swill the juices with a wineglassful of Madeira, removing as much fat as possible, and blend with the *demi-glace* or Espagnole sauce (see page 20). Two minutes before removing the sautéed vegetables from the stove, add the truffle, finely sliced. Place the chicken on a heated serving dish, arrange the vegetables carefully around. Taste the sauce for seasoning, pour over the chicken, decorate with pastry crescents, and serve at once. Have all the constituents of this dish ready and hot, to put together at the final moment – the chicken, vegetables, sauce and pastry crescents. Serves 4–6.

# Pheasant Mandarin

This dish is not, as the name might suggest, Chinese, but a French preparation of sautéed pheasant with mandarin oranges.

2 *pheasants*                     1 *wine glass of brandy*
2 *or 3 mandarins or*          *demi-glace sauce*
  *clementines*

Joint the pheasants, and sauté them in butter. Sauté the legs for 10 minutes or so before adding the breasts, as the legs take longer to cook. When the pheasants are tender, after about 30–40 minutes, remove and put them on a serving dish in a warm place. Swill the sauté pan with brandy, skim off the fat, and add the *demi-glace*. Quickly grate the peel of the oranges into the sauce while it is heating, using a fine grater. When the sauce is ready, pour over the pheasant, and serve decorated with quarters of the fruit. Serves 4.

# Quails in Aspic

A very impressive dish, but one that takes some time to prepare. Mrs Bridges seems to have had time, for many guests have spoken of her Quails in Aspic, as much an attraction to Eaton Place as the Bellamys themselves.

| | |
|---|---|
| 8 *quail* | *aspic jelly* |
| 4 *oz minced veal* | 1 *egg white* |
| 4 *oz pâté de foie gras truffé* | *cream* |
| *brown chaudfroid sauce* | *salt and pepper* |

The quails have to be stuffed, and to stuff them they have to be boned. Make a slit along the length of the backbone of each quail. With a sharp pointed knife lift the meat away either side of the carcass. Cut through the leg and wing joints, taking care not to break the skin, and cut the backbone away from the carcass, lifting it out. Not all the bones need be removed (it would take the hand of a Swiss brain surgeon) but sufficient to make a cavity for the forcemeat.

To make the forcemeat stuffing, pass the veal through as fine a mincer as possible – it should almost be a paste. Season with salt and pepper, mix with the stiffly beaten egg white, and a little thick cream. Chill for about 30 minutes. Add to this the pâté and mix well together. Stuff each bird with the forcemeat, and reshape them. Wrap each quail in a piece of damp cloth or muslin, so they retain their shape while poaching.

Put them in an ovenproof dish with a lid, cover with veal stock, and poach at 325° for 40 minutes. Test with a fine skewer to see if they are tender. Take the quails and unwrap them, and leave to cool. Now coat each quail with a brown Chaudfroid Sauce (see page 27) and decorate with diamonds of poached egg white and thinly sliced black truffle. Cover each quail with aspic jelly, and serve surrounded by chopped aspic. Serves 4.

# Caneton Sauvage au Porto

Wild duck has a strong flavour, and is generally served underdone. It can be soaked for an hour in salt water, or blanched for a few minutes in boiling, salted water prior to cooking, in order to make the taste milder. If you prefer duck 'overcooked', give it a further 20 minutes in the oven. Because the breasts cook more quickly than the rest of the duck, they can be removed and kept warm, and the duck returned to the oven to complete the cooking.

| | |
|---|---|
| 2 *wild ducks* | *thyme and parsley* |
| 4 *slices streaky bacon* | *salt and cayenne pepper* |
| *a large glass Port wine* | 1 *orange and* $\frac{1}{2}$ *lemon* |
| 1 *oz flour* | $\frac{1}{2}$ *pint game stock* |
| 1 *oz butter* | |

Make a Port Wine Sauce as on page 32, or as follows: Put the butter and flour in a saucepan, and cook very gently until it colours a golden brown. Add, by degrees, the game stock, stirring continuously. Boil the Port wine with the orange juice, the zest cut in fine strips, the juice of the lemon, a sprig of thyme and chopped parsley until it has reduced by half. Strain, and pour it into the sauce. Taste for seasoning. Cover the breasts of the ducks with bacon, and roast them at 425° for 20 minutes, remove the bacon and cook a further 10 minutes. Remove and slice the breasts, return the duck to the oven. After a further 20 minutes, remove and carve the legs. Add the juices to the sauce, and skim any fat, add the strips of orange peel. Serve the ducks decorated with slices of orange and watercress, accompanied by game chips and red cabbage. Serves 4.

# Game Pie

This is a raised pie with a crisp, rich, butter crust Mrs Bridges fashioned in the manner of a pork pie, but the crust differs by not being hot water pastry, as is usual with raised pies. Her game pie was in great demand at Eaton Place during the game season, where it was a speciality at luncheon parties. 'Watercress, redcurrant jelly and good Burgundy wine. There was always plenty of pie in quantity and it was well praised.'
The proportions here are for an 8-inch hinged pie mould, which will produce a 5 lb pie to serve 10–12.

For the crust:

| | |
|---|---|
| 10 *oz plain flour* | 1 *level teaspoon salt* |
| 5 *oz butter* | *about 2 tablespoons* |
| 2 *egg yolks* | *iced water* |

70

Sift flour and salt together. Cut the butter into small pieces and work it into the flour, until the consistency of fine crumbs. Add the two egg yolks and sufficient iced water to make a stiff dough. Knead the dough until smooth, and leave to rest in a cool place for an hour or more.

For the filling:

1 *lb minced veal seasoned with*     8 *oz ham*
    *salt, pepper and mixed herbs*     *aspic jelly*
2 *rashers finely chopped bacon*
*cooked and uncooked meat*
    *from any game*

Roll out the pastry dough to $\frac{1}{8}$ or $\frac{3}{16}$-inch thick, and cut pieces to fit the top, bottom and sides of the mould – the top oval being slightly larger than the bottom. Moisten the edges with a pastry brush and fit the pieces together in the mould; they must be well sealed not to let the juices escape. Put all of the veal forcemeat at the bottom of the pie, then a layer of ham, and a layer of the game meat cut into strips, another layer of ham, and game to fill the pie. Sprinkle with bacon. Put a pastry lid on top, and make a small hole in the centre. Decorate with pastry leaves, and glaze with egg and milk wash. Bake in a moderate oven, 375° for 1 hour. The pie is cooked when liquid begins to bubble in the vent. Do not remove from mould until the pie is cold, then invert to drain off juices. Finally, fill the pie with liquid aspic, and leave to set.

# Roast Grouse

Wipe the grouse, and season them with salt and pepper. Put some minced beef, or an ounce of butter inside the bird, as they have a tendency towards dryness. Wrap each grouse in streaky bacon, and roast, breast down, in a fairly hot oven, about 425–450° for 20 to 30 minutes, according to size. Remove the bacon 5 minutes before they are done, and dredge the birds with flour, basting frequently in order to brown them. While the birds are roasting, prepare a canapé by lightly frying the liver in bacon fat, mashing it with a fork, and working together with butter, salt and cayenne pepper. Spread this mixture on squares of fried bread or toast, and place under the grouse for the last few minutes of cooking. Serve the grouse on the canapés with the usual accompaniments.

# Braised or Stoved Grouse

'I am told,' says Mrs Bridges, 'that ovens are infrequently met with in Scotland, and people cook on top of the fire. Stoved grouse are not quite the same as braised grouse, because in Scotland they are cooked in a closed pot on top of the stove, which is why they are so called.'

Anyway, it is difficult to detect the difference between the two methods so far as flavour is concerned.

Brown the grouse in bacon fat with a teaspoonful of brown sugar. Slice two or three rashers of bacon, a small onion and a carrot, and fry together for 5 minutes. Put the grouse and the vegetables in a casserole and add a little stock or water. Cook in a moderate oven, or over a low flame for $1\frac{1}{2}$ hours, or until the grouse is tender. Check now and then to see that the bird is not burning, adding more stock or water as required.

# Roast Partridge

Partridge are in season from September 1st until February 1st. They are at their best during October and November, and need to be hung only a few days. Choose young birds for roasting. Place a knob of seasoned butter inside each bird, and wrap in bacon. Roast in a hot oven or on a spit for 30 minutes, basting frequently with butter. Flour 5 minutes before serving, and baste to brown.

# Partridge Pie

Split the partridges, and fry for 5 minutes in butter. Place them in a pie dish with one veal cutlet per bird, and a little chopped cooked ham. Season with salt and pepper, add a sprig or two of thyme and parsley. Add also some peeled button mushrooms, or sliced field mushrooms, and enough veal stock to cover. Prepare sufficient puff pastry to cover the pie dish – a large pie dish with a capacity of 5 pints would take three brace of partridges, $\frac{1}{2}$ lb mushrooms, about $1\frac{1}{2}$ pints of stock, and 1 lb pastry. Glaze the pastry with egg and milk wash, and bake in a hot oven 425° for 10 minutes, then at 350° for a further 40 minutes. Serves 8–10.

# Sussex Partridge Pudding

One of Mrs Harcourt's specialities. Mrs Bridges would have learned the recipe from her teacher at Southwold, for Mrs Harcourt was a Sussex woman, and Sussex is the 'true home of the suet pudding'.

Line a 2-pint pudding basin with 12 oz suet crust. Joint a brace of partridges, season with salt and black pepper, and add chopped parsley and a sprig of thyme. Fill the basin with some thinly sliced rump steak, the partridge joints, and sliced mushrooms, all dredged with flour. Pour in enough stock to almost fill the basin, and cover with a lid of suet crust, making sure the edges are well sealed. Cover with greaseproof paper and a cloth, and tie securely. Lower into a pan of boiling water, and simmer for at least 5 hours, but 6 to 8 hours is ideal. Serves 4–6.

# Jugged Hare

Cut the hare into joints, dredge them in flour and season with salt and pepper. Fry them in bacon fat until lightly browned. Put the joints in a tall ovenproof pot with a close-fitting lid, add 2 medium-sized, sliced onions, and a sliced carrot. Peel a small onion, stick it with 5 or 6 cloves, and put this in the pot with the rest. Add 6 whole mushrooms, 2 chopped slices of streaky bacon, 3 or 4 peppercorns, and a bouquet garni. Cover with a good, rich stock, and add a full glass of red wine. Cover the pot, and set to cook either in a *bain-marie* over the fire, or in the oven. Give the hare 3 hours, and check to see if it is tender. Now add a glass of Port which you have simmered in a pan with a tablespoonful of redcurrant jelly.

At this point in the cooking you may add the blood of the hare, usually reserved to thicken the gravy, but do not allow it to boil, otherwise the gravy will curdle. Serve with forcemeat balls and redcurrant jelly. Make the forcemeat balls with 6 oz breadcrumbs, a handful of chopped parsley, 2 oz shredded suet, salt and pepper. Bind this mixture with an egg, adding a little milk if needed. Roll into small balls, and bake in a moderate oven for 30 minutes, or fry in bacon fat or dripping until browned. Serves 6–8.

# Venison

Venison should hang for about two weeks, and be examined and carefully wiped each day. Because venison is inclined to toughness, the cuts served at Eaton Place were always marinated in red wine, to which Mrs Bridges added a chopped onion, a bay leaf or two, rosemary and crushed juniper berries. The meat was left to marinate overnight, and then larded with bacon fat. The best cuts are the haunch, loin and fillet. The usual accompaniments include gravy, Cumberland Sauce (see page 28), redcurrant jelly, purée of chestnuts, braised celery.

To roast a haunch of venison, cover it with well-buttered greaseproof paper, then with a stiff paste of flour mixed with enough water and fat to bind it together. Cover with more paper, and secure with string. (Today, it would be sufficient to butter the haunch, and wrap it in baking foil.)

Roast the meat from 3 to 5 hours, calculating about 15 minutes to the pound. Half an hour before you wish to serve, remove the paper and paste, or the foil, and dredge with flour. Baste now and then with butter, until the meat is well browned.

# GAME AND POULTRY

## The Downstairs Recipes

Chicken Pie
Pigeon Pie
Pigeon Pudding
Pigeon Pie with a suet crust
Rook Pie
Lemon Chicken
Southwold Rabbit Pie
Rabbit in Cider

# Chicken Pie

4 lb roasting chicken or
   boiling fowl
1 large onion
parsley, bay leaves, thyme
$\frac{1}{2}$ lb mushrooms
egg and milk

cream
puff pastry
flour and butter to make
   a roux
salt, pepper

Simmer the chicken in water to cover, with the onion, a bunch of parsley and a bay leaf, until tender. Mrs Bridges always used an old boiling fowl for this dish, which would have taken perhaps 2 hours. A roasting bird will be tender in about an hour. Remove the chicken, and strain the stock into a pan, bring to the boil and reduce until you have a $\frac{1}{2}$ pint of stock. Peel the meat from the bones, slicing any large pieces, and place them in a pie dish. Add a bay leaf and a sprig of thyme, season with salt and pepper. Make a roux with flour and butter, and add the reduced stock by degrees, until the sauce is smooth. It may be thinned if needed with a little milk. Add a spoonful of cream, and pour the sauce over the chicken. This sauce should be not too thick, but the consistency of single cream. Sprinkle with chopped parsley, and cover with sliced mushrooms. Cover the pie dish with puff pastry, and glaze with egg and milk wash. Put in a hot oven, 425° for 10 minutes, or until the crust has risen. Turn the heat down to 350° and finish cooking for a further 30 minutes, until the crust is golden brown. Serves 6–8.

# Pigeon Pie

'The country folk where I was brought up made pies from all manner of birds,' writes Mrs Bridges, 'from young rooks and from blackbirds, like in the nursery rhyme. When they made a pigeon pie, they always baked it with the feet of the birds sticking through the crust. That simply would not do in a good kitchen!'

1 lb lean beef steak
4 plump pigeons
4 oz mushrooms
1 oz flour
egg and milk

8 oz shortcrust pastry
2 bay leaves
$\frac{1}{2}$ pint brown stock
salt, pepper, mace

Cut the steak in slices, and roll them in seasoned flour. Lay them on the bottom of a pie dish. Slice the breasts from the pigeons, dust with flour, and put them on the steak. Chop the mushrooms and put them in with the meat, also the bay leaves and mace. Cover with stock, then with the pastry, brushed with egg glaze. Bake at 425° for 30 minutes, then reduce the heat and cook for a further hour. Cover the pie with foil or greaseproof paper after the first 30 minutes, to prevent the pastry from burning and getting too hard. Serves 4–6.

# Pigeon Pudding

This recipe is the same as the Sussex Partridge Pudding in the Upstairs section, substituting pigeons for partridges. Ideally, the pigeons should be part roasted for 15 minutes, and the meat cut from the carcasses, and the juices added to the stock. Failing this, split each pigeon in half, and remove the legs.

# Pigeon Pie with a suet crust

4 *plump pigeons*
½ *lb beef steak*
¼ *lb mushrooms*
1 *small onion*
3–4 *rashers streaky bacon*

1 *bay leaf, cloves, mace*
*suet crust (see recipe for*
    *Steak and Kidney Pudding)*
*salt and pepper*

Joint the pigeons, removing the breasts and legs, and put the carcasses to simmer in 1 pint of water, with an onion, salt and pepper, 2 cloves and a tiny piece of mace. Boil and skim, until a rich stock has been obtained, and thicken it with a roux, or some flour and a little Bisto powder mixed with dripping and fried for a moment. Take a pie dish large enough to hold all the ingredients. Slice the beef steak very thinly, and lay at the bottom of the dish. Cover it with the pigeon pieces, the bacon chopped into small squares and the mushrooms, peeled and sliced. Season well, place a bay leaf in the centre, and cover with some of the gravy. Now cover the whole with suet crust, rolled to a ¼ inch thickness. Cover the dish with greaseproof paper (or with foil) and bake for an hour at 375°. The crust should be light as fresh bread and well risen. Before serving, cut a piece from the crust, and pour in the rest of the hot gravy. Serves 4–6.

# Rook Pie

'There was a warrener in Southwold who had permission to thin
out the rookeries and sell the rooks locally. Rook pie was always
made on the farms in early summer, and the best I ever tasted
was at a farm wedding in 1875, or thereabouts. There was a cold
sauced lemon chicken, and I had the recipe for both.'

| | |
|---|---|
| 6 *young rooks* | *puff pastry* |
| 1 *lb rump steak* | *thyme and parsley* |
| 3 *rashers bacon* | *salt and pepper* |
| ½ *pint beef stock or good gravy* | *egg* |

'You don't pluck young rooks, you skin them, cutting the skin
near the thighs and drawing it back over the head. Also, you have
to take the backbone out, as it is inclined towards bitterness.'
Draw and split the birds, remove head and neck of each and also
the backbone. Cut the beefsteak into thin slices and arrange them
on the bottom of a pie dish. Place the pieces of rook on the beef,
then the bacon, diced. Place a sprig or two of thyme in the dish,
and a sprinkling of chopped parsley. Season well with salt and
pepper, add the gravy or stock to cover the meat. With a good
puff pastry, cover the pie dish, glaze with beaten egg, and bake
in a hot oven (425°) for 20 minutes. Place a piece of greaseproof
paper over the pastry, turn the oven down low (325–350°) and
bake a further 1½ hours, removing the paper for the final 10
minutes – unless the pastry is well browned. Serves 4–6.

# Lemon Chicken

This is a fine picnic dish, very popular in the early 1900s. Stuff
a chicken with an onion and breadcrumb mixture, bound with
an egg, well seasoned, and with a good bunch of lemon thyme
chopped and added to the mixture. Roast in the usual way, and
allow to get cold. Skin the chicken, otherwise it will 'cut un-
comfortably' and cover it with a thick, creamy Béchamel, made
with chicken stock and cream, into which you grate the rind of a
lemon. Decorate the chicken as you will. Serves 4–6.

# Southwold Rabbit Pie

'Pegler, the warrener, who cleared out the rooks, had permission from Harris (the head keeper at Southwold) to ferret for rabbits on the estate, by which means they were kept down. My Rabbit Pie was very popular with the staff.'

| | |
|---|---|
| 2 *rabbits* | *mixed dried herbs* |
| 4 *oz smoked bacon* | 1 *egg* |
| 2 *medium size onions* | 1 *glass claret* |
| *a small pippin apple* | $\frac{3}{4}$ *pint stock* |
| *(finely chopped)* | *puff pastry* |
| 2 *oz white breadcrumbs* | *salt and pepper* |
| *egg and milk* | |

Joint the rabbits. Take the liver and kidneys and chop them finely, also the apple. Make a forcemeat with the liver and kidneys, the breadcrumbs, a sprinkling of herbs, the apple, salt and pepper, and the egg to make the mixture bind. Roll the mixture into small forcemeat balls. Place the rabbit, the bacon cut into small pieces, the onions finely sliced, and the forcemeat balls in a pie dish of sufficient size. Season well with salt and pepper, add another dash of dried herbs. Mix the wine with the stock, and pour over the meat. Cover with good puff pastry, decorate the top with pastry leaves, and glaze with beaten egg mixed with milk. Bake for 20 minutes at 425°, until the pastry is risen, then cover with paper or foil, and bake a further hour and 10 minutes. For the final 10 minutes of cooking, remove the paper, unless the pastry is well browned. Serves 6–8.


# Rabbit in Cider

| | |
|---|---|
| *a young and tender rabbit* | 1 *pint dry cider* |
| $\frac{1}{4}$ *lb green bacon* | *flour* |
| *a large onion* | *salt, pepper, bay leaves,* |
| 2 *medium carrots* | *parsley, thyme* |
| *a stalk of celery* | |

Joint the rabbit, cut the bacon into small pieces. Fry the bacon in oil or good quality dripping for a few minutes, but do not allow it to become crisp. Remove the bacon, add the pieces of rabbit well floured and seasoned. Fry them until they are lightly browned. Put the bacon and rabbit into a stewpan, draining off excess fat. Chop the onion, slice the carrots, cut the celery into

small pieces, fry these gently for 10 minutes, and add them to the meat. Tie parsley and thyme in a bunch (or use a *bouquet garni* in muslin) and place in the stewpan along with 2 bay leaves. Add the cider and stew for an hour in a covered pan over a moderate heat. Test now and then to see that the rabbit is not overcooked. This depends, of course, on the age of the rabbit; a young one will take about 1 hour, an old one about 2 hours. At the end of the cooking, the liquid should be reduced to half its original quantity, to produce a sauce the consistency of thin cream. Sprinkle chopped parsley on the dish before serving. Serves 4.

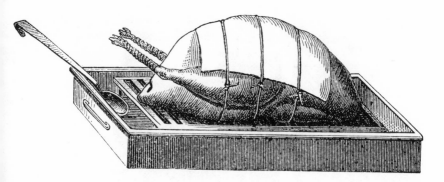

# MEAT

The Edwardians were very partial to mutton, and epicures insisted that a sheep be five years and over before it possessed enough flavour. Today, everything is 'lamb', but Mrs Bridges would have made the distinction between lamb and mutton, preferring to use the larger joints of mutton for roasting. Her Baron of Mutton was particularly esteemed at Eaton Place, and when it came to roasting meats, she had no equal; Baron of Mutton was one of the dishes served to Edward VII when he came for dinner with the Bellamys.

We were a great nation of meat eaters, and we liked our meat to have a flavour. Mrs Bridges devotes nearly ten pages to a description of the various types of cattle, sheep and pigs, to Southdown sheep, Hereford bulls, and acorn-fed pigs of the forests – alas, no more. We enjoyed the dark, almost gamey taste of mature mutton, the red, juicy tenderness of well-hung beef, insisting on the traditional accompaniments to heighten flavour: Horseradish, Mustard, Harvey's Sauce and Lea & Perrins' Worcestershire Sauce, Mint Sauce and Caper Sauce, and plenty of rich gravy. Variety of cuts was limited to joints, chops and steaks, roasted or grilled, served with boiled vegetables swimming in butter – that was how men at the turn of the century preferred to eat.

But the French influence could not be ignored. The great chef Escoffier had recently arrived in ⸢London, and had served frogs' legs to the Prince of Wales, who was himself no stranger to the Paris fashions of the day. Across the Channel chefs were cooking tournedos in butter, and placing them on croûtons of fried bread, with a glistening sauce and an imaginative garnish.

English chefs added the new, fashionable creations to their repertoire, Tournedos Rossini, Langtry, Lakmé, Melba, and Sarah Bernhardt; to which Mrs Bridges, not to be outdone, added her own contribution in honour of her employer: Tournedos Bellamy, placed on a croûton covered with foie gras, garnished with artichoke bottoms stuffed with mushroom purée, served with a Sauce Choron!

During the Season, luncheon parties were all the rage, and hostesses provided dainty dishes for their guests, dishes which bore such titles as 'Little Bombs of Veal à la Gêlée', and 'Little Nectarines of Foie Gras à la Belle'. A cook was expected to produce any number of these tedious little offerings at the drop of a spoon. 'They are,' said Mrs Bridges, 'troublesome to prepare, and divert a cook's attention from the important ⸤asks at hand.' Nevertheless, she felt obliged to give no fewer than seventy-two recipes for the benefit of her readers.

Like a long-distance runner, Mrs Bridges kept her strength in reserve. A request from 'upstairs' for something special sent her bustling to the stove to make Côtes de Veau Talleyrand – veal cutlets spread with chicken forcemeat, rolled in chopped truffles, garnished with macaroni mixed with foie gras and truffles, and served with a Sauce Perigueux. But, as Mrs Bridges said, '. . . it is in the simple things that one's true skill and honest application are revealed,' adding the little homily, 'The secret of success is constancy of purpose.'

Although she does not say so, it is certain that similar tastes were shared both upstairs and downstairs, and that master and servant alike enjoyed Mrs Bridges' Cottage Pie, Hot Pot, Steak and Kidney Pudding, Boiled Beef and Carrots, Toad-in-the-Hole, and the sweet, steamed puddings that went to the table covered in jam or custard. After all, an abundance of rich food would have contradicted Victorian observance of thrift and parsimony. Portions, though, and cuts of meat, tended to be large, because the Victorians and Edwardians went in for large families. There were always plenty of leftovers, and inventive cooks turned these into tasty réchauffé dishes, *kromeskies*, rissoles, pâtés and so on.

# MEAT

## The Upstairs Recipes

Tournedos Bellamy
Tournedos Médicis
Tournedos Henry IV
Tournedos Rossini
Filet de Boeuf Froid
    Montlhéry
Filet de Boeuf en
    Croûte 'Excellence'
Côtes de Veau
    Talleyrand
Médaillons de Veau
    à la Crème
Médaillons de Veau
    Marie Louise
Médaillons de Veau
    Zingara
Longe de Veau
    Bordelaise
Côtelettes d'Agneau
    en Papillotes
Lamb Cutlets King
    Charles
Côtelettes d'Agneau
    Cyrano
Noisettes d'Agneau
    à la Belgrave

Noisettes d'Agneau
    Langtry
Gigot Rôti à la
    Richelieu
Baked Ham with
    Champagne Sauce
Jambon à la
    Bigarrade
Soufflé de Jambon
Ris de Veau
    Gladstone

# Tournedos Bellamy

tournedos steaks (1 per
  person)
slices of white bread, cut in
  circles (1 per steak)
butter

pâté de foie gras (tinned)
artichoke bottoms
mushrooms for purée
sauce Choron

Sauté the tournedos gently in butter, until they are cooked
according to preference. Ideally the steak should be served rare.
Each tournedo is placed on a circle of bread, which has been cut
slightly larger than the steak, fried in butter, and spread with
foie gras.
Make a mushroom purée by sautéing them in butter until they
are soft, passing them through a fine sieve and mixing with
stiff double cream. Season with salt. Plunge the artichoke bottoms into boiling water for a few moments, drain, and fill each
with mushroom purée, arrange round the tournedos – 4 stuffed
artichokes to each steak, and serve with Sauce Choron (see
page 28).

# Tournedos Médicis

tournedos steaks
artichoke bottoms
fresh petits pois
new carrots

noisette potatoes
Madeira half-glaze
Béarnaise sauce

The steaks are cooked as the previous recipe, with a garnish of
artichoke bottoms, peas, carrots shaped into tiny balls, noisette
potatoes, and served with two sauces – the Béarnaise by the side
of the vegetables, the Madère on the steak.

# Tournedos Henry IV

tournedos steaks
croûtons of fried bread

Béarnaise Sauce
pont-neuf potatoes

In this recipe the tournedos are grilled, and should be grilled over
charcoal, although this is not essential. Place each steak on a
circle of fried bread, and pipe a ring of Béarnaise round the top of
each steak, just on the edge. Serve with pont-neuf potatoes (see
page 122).

# Tournedos Rossini

*tournedos steaks*  
*croûtons*  
*meat glaze*  
*pâté de foie gras*

*truffles*  
*Madeira*  
*demi-glace sauce*

The steaks are sautéed in butter, and placed on croûtons of bread fried in butter and moistened with meat glaze. 'The great mistake with Tournedos Rossini,' writes Mrs Bridges, 'is in allowing the croûtons to become soggy, either with too much meat glaze, or through juices coming from the steak.' Sauté a disc of foie gras, cut to fit on top of the steak, in butter for a few minutes, and set it on top of the steak. Decorate with a slice of truffle. The steak is served with a *demi-glace* sauce, flavoured with Madeira.

# Filet de Boeuf Froid Montlhéry

*1 lb fillet beef, in one piece*  
*2 pints aspic jelly*  
*small piece of truffle, or*  
   *truffle peelings*  
*mayonnaise*

*French beans, macedoine of*  
   *carrots, turnips and peas,*  
   *artichoke bottoms, asparagus*  
   *tips*

The fillet is cooked, left to get cold, and cut into slices. (Tie the fillet with string to keep it in shape while cooking, the aim is to achieve nicely rounded slices.) Cook in a hot oven, 425° for about 30 minutes, basting occasionally with beef dripping. Leave until quite cold, remove the string, and cut the fillet into slices of $\frac{1}{2}$-inch thickness. Trim each piece carefully, and lay it separately in a shallow baking tin or sandwich tin, and decorate with truffles in thin slivers and cut in the shape of lozenges or diamonds. Gently spoon cool aspic, not yet at setting point, into the tin and cover the slices to a depth of $\frac{1}{4}$ inch. When the aspic has set, cut around each fillet with a knife or shaped cutter, and lift on to a serving dish. Prepare a macedoine of cold, cooked carrots and turnips, cut into tiny cubes. Mix with peas, and cohere with mayonnaise. Coat a number of timbale moulds with aspic, and fill with macedoine.

Take some artichoke bottoms, place two asparagus tips in each, and coat with aspic, Boil some French beans in salted water, leave them to get cold, and mix them with a spoonful of good olive oil, until they glisten. The fillets de boeuf Montlhéry are sent to the table decorated by the timbales of vegetables, the artichoke bottoms and the French beans. Chopped aspic is arranged around, and mayonnaise served with the dish. Serves 6.

# Filet de Boeuf en Croûte 'Excellence'

2 lb fillet beef
4 oz foie gras
puff pastry, about ½ to ¾ lb
egg and milk

watercress
demi-glace sauce

Carefully trim the fillet, and tie it with string to keep its shape while cooking. Roast in a hot oven, basting now and then with butter, for 10 minutes. Allow the fillet to get cold. Spread the entire fillet with the foie gras, and encase it in puff pastry, as follows: roll out the pastry and cut into two rectangles, one piece smaller by about a third. Place the beef on the larger piece, and bring the sides up. Moisten the edges, place the other piece on top, and seal the edges. Close the ends, turn the whole package over, and decorate with pastry leaves and fleurons. Glaze with beaten egg and milk, and bake in an oven set at 425°, for 30 minutes, or until the pastry is well risen and browned. To serve, cut into slices, decorate with watercress, and serve each slice masked with demi-glace sauce (see page 25). Serves 6.

# Côtes de Veau Talleyrand

10 veal cutlets
1 lb fresh chicken meat
4 eggs
4 oz double cream
chopped truffles

butter
4 oz foie gras
8 oz macaroni
3 oz Gruyère cheese

Make a forcemeat by passing the chicken meat through a fine sieve, food mill or in a blender. Season with salt and pepper, and add the whites of two eggs – reserving the yolks – by degrees until well blended. Chill for at least 2 hours. Now incorporate the cream, beaten until thick, with the forcemeat. The finished forcemeat should be smooth, and of sufficient consistency to hold its shape, so take care with the quantity of cream added. Trim the cutlets, cook them gently in butter, and allow to cool. Spread both sides of each with a quantity of the forcemeat, sufficient to give shape to the cutlets, and dip them in beaten egg yolks to which you have added an extra two whole eggs. Coat each cutlet on both sides with finely chopped truffles, and return to the pan to finish cooking in the butter – about 5 minutes each side.

The cutlets are served with a Talleyrand garnish. Cook the macaroni in boiling, salted water to the *al dente* stage, still firm enough to bite into and not overcooked and soft. Drain quickly, and mix with butter and grated Gruyère cheese. Add diced foie gras and thin strips of truffle to the macaroni, and arrange on a heated platter with the cutlets. Accurate synchronising of the various parts of this dish is essential, so have the foie gras and truffle ready to incorporate with the pasta, and keep the cutlets in a warm place, or arrange it that the cutlets finish cooking at the same moment as the macaroni. Cutlets Talleyrand are to be sent to the table hot, with a Sauce Périgueux ready at the side. (See page 31.) Serves 5.

# Médaillons or Noisettes de Veau

The finest part of the veal fillet, trimmed round and sautéed in butter, prepared with various garnishes and sauces. With the term 'veal fillet', a problem arises. The French *filet* and the English fillet are different cuts of meat, and cook differently. *Filet de veau* is cut from the underside of the loin, while veal fillet is cut from the leg. Mrs Bridges was a valuable customer to her butcher, and she insisted on the French cuts, since she was preparing French dishes. If your butcher refuses to undercut the loin, ask for the leg *filet* in one piece, and cut médaillons according to the thickness you desire.

*Filet de veau* needs only 10 to 15 minutes sautéing, while veal fillet requires about 20 to 25 minutes to cook to the right point of tenderness.

# Médaillons de Veau à la Crème

Sauté the médaillons in butter, remove from the pan, and put in a warm place. Swill the pan with single cream, scraping any bits in the pan, blending the juices and butter with the cream. Add a good squeeze of lemon juice, pour over the médaillons, and serve.

# Marie Louise

Dip each médaillon in beaten egg, then coat in fine breadcrumbs. Sauté in butter until golden, and serve with artichoke
bottoms filled with a mixture of mushroom purée and soubise
purée. Chop the mushrooms finely, sauté in butter for a few
minutes, and pass them through a fine sieve. For the soubise
purée, slice a large onion, blanch it in boiling water, and cook it
in butter in a covered pan until soft. Do not allow it to
colour. Now bind the onions with a thick Béchamel Sauce,
season with salt, pepper and nutmeg, cook for a further 5
minutes, stirring frequently. Pass through a fine sieve, and blend
with the mushroom purée. Serve with a thickened gravy, made
from the butter in which you have cooked the médaillons, add a
spoonful of cornflour and sufficient veal or chicken stock to make
a nice gravy. Season, and pour over the veal.

# Zingara

Cook as in the above recipe and garnish with ham, mushrooms
and truffles, cut into fine julienne strips, sautéed in butter until
soft, flavoured with chopped fresh tarragon leaves, and bound
with a *demi-glace* sauce to which is added a little tomato purée
and a half glass of Madeira. Serve the sauce separately with the
veal. The recipe for Zingara Sauce is on page 32.

# Longe de Veau Bordelaise

| | |
|---|---|
| *loin of veal* | *a dozen artichoke bottoms* |
| 3 *medium carrots* | 1 *lb flat noodles, cooked* |
| 2 *Spanish onions* | *butter* |
| 1 *lb flat-topped field* | *parsley* |
| *mushrooms, not too large* | *salt and pepper* |

Bone and roll the loin of veal, tying it with string at intervals
along its length. Brown it gently in good dripping. Scrape the
carrots and slice them in rounds. Peel and slice the onions, and
add carrots and onions to the meat. Season well. Cook until the
vegetables are also browned, transfer to an ovenproof dish with
a lid, a casserole or cocotte. Add a quarter pint of water, cover
and cook in the oven at 350° until the meat is tender. It will take
about 2 hours. Sauté the mushrooms whole in butter and also the

artichoke bottoms, cut into quarters. Put the veal on a bed of noodles, and arrange the vegetables around. Déglacé the cocotte and pour it over the meat. Garnish with chopped parsley. Serves 6–8.

# Côtelettes d'Agneau en Papillotes

8 *lamb chops, two per person*
$\frac{1}{2}$ *lb mushrooms*
4 *oz cooked ham, sliced thinly*
*breadcrumbs from a thick*
   *slice of white bread*
*parsley*
*speck of garlic*

*tomato purée*
$\frac{1}{2}$ *breakfastcupful stock*
*butter*
*salt, pepper*
*greaseproof paper or foil*
*Sauce Madère*

Trim the chops, and cook them in butter, 3 minutes each side. Put them to one side, in a warm place, and make the *duxelles* garnish: slice the mushrooms finely, and cook them in butter until soft. Add the breadcrumbs, a little chopped parsley, garlic, salt and pepper, a teaspoonful of tomato purée, and moisten with stock to achieve a thick paste. Cut heart shapes from the paper or foil, as many shapes as you have chops and of sufficient size to enclose them. Spread the *duxelles* mixture on one side of each chop, then a piece of ham shaped to cover. Lay this down on one side of the paper, leaving the undressed side of the chop uppermost. Spread this side with the paste, and cover with ham. Fold the remaining half of the paper heart to meet the edges, and crimp them tightly. Put the papillotes in an oven set at 400°, and cook them for 20 minutes, or until the paper browns. Have the Sauce Madère ready, take the chops in their cases and place them on each guest's plate to unwrap. This is part of the presentation of papillotes, and it is why greaseproof paper is more acceptable than foil. 'At one time,' Mrs Bridges informs us, 'the paper cases were made of parchment. It is an ancient French recipe, or so I was taught.' The sauce should be poured over the chops as soon as they are opened, for the ham quickly dries, and curls at the edges, spoiling the effect.

95

# Lamb Cutlets King Charles

8 *lamb cutlets*
1 *lb onions*
2 *oz rice*

*teacup of stock*
*butter*
1 *egg*

With the onions and rice, make a soubise purée as follows: slice the onions finely in butter until soft. Add the rice, well washed, and the stock. Simmer until the rice is cooked, adding more stock if required. Season well with salt and pepper, and press through a fine sieve, or purée in a blender. The result should be of a thick consistency.

Cook one side of each cutlet in butter, 4–5 minutes. Spread with the soubise purée, brush with beaten egg. Put the cutlets back in the cooking pan dressed side uppermost, and sauté them in butter. Finish them off by glazing under a grill.

# Côtelettes d'Agneau Cyrano

A very impressive way of serving cutlets in the form of a crown, decorated with croûtons and artichoke bottoms stuffed with *foie gras*.

2 *whole best ends of neck*
16 *artichoke bottoms*
12 *oz foie gras*
*truffles*

*butter*
*bread for croûtons*
*salt, pepper*
*Châteaubriand Sauce*

Cut the cutlets from the joints, and trim them; there should be 16 in all. The dish can be made with half that quantity but, as Mrs Bridges says, 'a whole crown has a more regal aspect'.

Season the cutlets, and cook them in butter. In another pan, fry some croûtons of white bread cut into heart shapes. Sauté the artichoke bottoms in butter, pass the *foie gras* through a fine sieve, finely slice the truffles. When the cutlets are cooked, arrange them on a serving dish in the shape of a crown, each standing on end, the rib bone uppermost and pointing outwards. In one or two circles around the crown, arrange alternately the croûtons, and the artichoke bottoms filled with foie gras. Place a slice of truffle on each pile of foie gras. Serve with a Châteaubriand Sauce. Serves 8–10.

# Noisettes d'Agneau à la Belgrave

Eaton Place is in Belgravia, but it is not certain that this dish is
an invention of Mrs Bridges, and named after the locality – she
was more in the habit of dedicating her culinary inventions to
persons, her 'Chicken Asquith' for example. Anyway, this is
quite an attractive way of presenting noisettes (the cutlets from
the best end, without the bone and trimmed).

| | |
|---|---|
| 8 *noisettes* | 4 *oz double cream* |
| *bread for croûtons* | *salt and pepper* |
| 2 *lb shelled green peas* | *Espagnole Sauce* |
| *butter* | *sherry* |

Season the noisettes, cook them in butter for 6 minutes; they
should be soft and tender and not overcooked. Place each on a
croûton of fried bread cut to the shape of the noisette. Spoon or
pipe round a purée of green peas, made by cooking the peas in
salted water until soft, and passing them through a fine sieve.
Add butter and enough thick double cream, to make a purée of
piping consistency. Serve with an Espagnole Sauce, flavoured
with sherry. It is optional to add a dessertspoonful of finely
chopped green olives to the sauce. Serves 4–6.

# Noisettes d'Agneau Langtry

'A new dish, named after the actress (Lily Langtry, the "Jersey
Lily") and a rather dressy one,' says Mrs Bridges tartly. Did she
mean the dish, or the actress, one wonders? It is, in fact, rather
a simple and attractive presentation, and probably invented by
Escoffier.

| | |
|---|---|
| *noisettes of lamb* | *chervil, salt and pepper* |
| *bread for croûtons* | *Perigueux Sauce* |
| *a tomato and an olive for* | |
| *each noisette* | |

The noisettes are cooked as in the previous recipe, and placed on
croûtons. Bake a small tomato in the oven until soft, and place
on the noisette, with a leaf of chervil, and a stoned black olive
on the tomato. Serve with a Périgueux Sauce (see page 31).

# Gigot Rôti à la Richelieu

It would appear that garlic was not very popular at Eaton Place, for Mrs Bridges makes scant reference to it, even in French dishes. It is usual to stud a leg of lamb with garlic before roasting, but this is omitted from her recipe, and the inclusion of garlic is a matter of personal taste. A joint of mutton was sent to the table with a soubise purée or sauce, and on special occasions a garnish of stuffed tomatoes and mushrooms.

Roast the joint at 375°, allowing 20 minutes to the pound, plus an extra 20 minutes, a 3 lb leg would thus take 1 hour 20 minutes to cook. Baste frequently with dripping during the roasting. A Richelieu garnish is made as follows: Take 8 large mushroom heads, and 8 medium tomatoes. Scoop the insides from the tomatoes, and stuff them and the mushrooms with vegetable *duxelles*: reduce $\frac{1}{4}$ bottle of dry white wine by half. Sauté 8 oz finely chopped mushrooms in butter until soft. Add a breakfast-cupful of white breadcrumbs, salt and pepper, chopped parsley, a speck of garlic, a teaspoonful of tomato purée, and sufficient gravy or stock to work into a fairly loose mixture, suitable for stuffing. Now fill the tomatoes and mushrooms with the mixture, coat with breadcrumbs, dot with butter, and bake in a moderate oven until tender. (Braised lettuce and new potatoes are other accompaniments to Richelieu.) Déglacé the roasting pan with dry white wine, work in some butter, and pour over the meat. Serves 6–8.

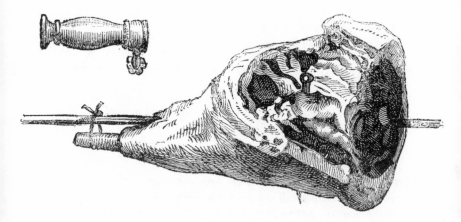

# Baked Ham with Champagne Sauce

It is likely that Escoffier had not invented his extravagant 'Jambon en Surprise' when Mrs Bridges' book was first published, although she does include a recipe for ham with champagne. Escoffier's offering was a York or Prague ham boiled in champagne, skinned and trimmed. A cup-sized piece was taken from the centre of the ham, and the hole filled with *foie gras* decorated with aspic and truffles; we may conclude that the surprise was the bill presented to the diner.

Mrs Bridges' recipe recommends boiling the ham in water, and finishing by baking, and basting with champagne.

| | |
|---|---|
| *a ham* | *spinach purée* |
| *meat glaze* | *Champagne Sauce* |
| *½ bottle of champagne* | |

Soak the ham in cold water overnight. Boil gently in water to cover, allowing 20 minutes per pound of ham. Take from the water, and allow to cool, Peel the skin from the ham, and trim the fat neatly, scoring across lattice-like with a sharp knife. Put it in a baking dish, and brush with a meat glaze. Bake at 425° until browned, and baste every now and then with champagne. Keep some of the champagne for the Sauce, which is merely a reduced Espagnole thinned with champagne (see page 27). Serve the ham with spinach purée.

# Jambon à la Bigarrade

Soak the ham overnight. Boil as in previous recipe, and trim the fat. Glaze with meat glaze, bake in an oven set at 425° for 30 minutes, basting with dry sherry. Serve with orange salad and a Sauce Bigarrade (see page 26).

# Soufflé de Jambon

This recipe utilises lean, cooked ham.

| | |
|---|---|
| 1 *lb cooked ham* | 8 *egg whites, stiffly beaten* |
| ½ *pint thick Béchamel Sauce* | *salt and cayenne pepper* |
| 5 *egg yolks* | |

Pass the ham, finely chopped, through a food mill, blender or sieve. Blend to a purée with the Béchamel Sauce. Season well, and add the egg yolks one by one. Fold in the whites and pour into a soufflé mould; if necessary tie a buttered band of grease-proof paper, 4 inches wide, round the top of the mould. Bake at 375° until well risen and brown – about 20–25 minutes. The soufflé is ready when it is soft in the centre – almost liquid – and cooked around the outside.

Add asparagus tips and sliced truffles to the mixture, and you have *Soufflé de Jambon Alexandra*. The moment the soufflé comes from the oven, decorate the top with a sprinkling of truffle shavings, and send quickly to the table. Serves 4–6.

# Ris de Veau Gladstone

When the Governor of the Bank of England, Samuel Stewart Gladstone, dined at Eaton Place, Mrs Bridges had planned the classic *Ris de Veau Financière*, requiring a garnish of *quenelles*, kidneys, truffles, mushrooms and cockscombs. But cockscombs were not available. 'I sent the servants to all quarters of London after cockscombs, but there were none to be had. You cannot make a Financière garnish *without* cockscombs,' she grumbled, 'a Financière *is*, or it *isn't!*' However, like all good cooks, she improvised, and thought it sufficiently acceptable to include in her book.

| | |
|---|---|
| 4 *sweetbreads* | ½ *pint brown stock* |
| 1 *calf's kidney* | 6 *blanched chestnuts* |
| 2 *carrots, a turnip, a small* | *a small truffle* |
| *onion, a stalk of celery* | ¼ *lb mushrooms* |
| *butter* | *Madeira wine* |

Soak the sweetbreads for 2 hours in water. Place in a pan with fresh water, and bring slowly to the boil, for 10 minutes. Drain, and plunge them into cold water. Remove any gristle or untidy pieces from the sweetbreads, and place them in a cocotte or casserole. Arrange round them the vegetables, sliced and sautéed for 10 minutes in butter. Slice the kidney and put it in with the sweetbreads. Blanch the chestnuts, having peeled them, by boiling for 5 minutes, plunging into cold water, draining and chopping coarsely. Peel the mushrooms, sauté them in butter for a few minutes (for this dish, choose button mushrooms, and merely wipe them, do not peel). Finely slice the truffle. Put everything in the cocotte with the stock, season well and put in an oven at 350° for 45 minutes.

Take the dish from the oven and strain the sauce, adding a glass of Madeira. Serve in the cocotte and pour the sauce over. If needed, the sauce may be thickened with a little arrowroot or cornflour. Serves 4.

# MEAT

## The Downstairs Recipes

Boiled Beef and
   Carrots
Cottage Pie
Boiled Gammon with
   Parsley Sauce
Lancashire Hot Pot
Irish Stew
Oxtail Braised with
   Parsnips
Steak and Kidney
   Pie
Steak and Kidney
   Pudding
Toad-in-the-Hole
Pork Pie
Brawn
Pig's Trotters
Tripe and Onions
Devilled Beef Bones
Steak and Onions
Stuffed Shoulder of
   Lamb (or Mutton)

# Boiled Beef and Carrots with Dumplings

In 1909 Harry Champion made popular the song, *Boiled beef and carrots*, and servants downstairs sang snatches of the lyrics. Kitchens rang with, *Don't eat like vegetarians on the stuff they give to parrots, Go out tonight and blow your kite on boiled beef and carrots.* The servants at Eaton Place would have had better reason to stay at home, for Mrs Bridges mentions that her boiled beef was constantly requested, especially during the winter months. This was her recipe:

*a 4 lb lean piece of salted
    silverside
an onion stuck with 2 or 3
    cloves
a dozen or so medium onions*

*a dozen carrots, whole if small,
    or quartered if large
3 parsnips, quartered
a bunch of parsley
a few peppercorns
an Oxo cube*

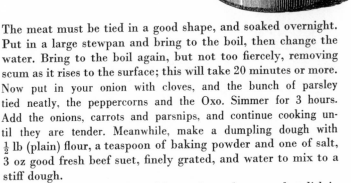

The meat must be tied in a good shape, and soaked overnight. Put in a large stewpan and bring to the boil, then change the water. Bring to the boil again, but not too fiercely, removing scum as it rises to the surface; this will take 20 minutes or more. Now put in your onion with cloves, and the bunch of parsley tied neatly, the peppercorns and the Oxo. Simmer for 3 hours. Add the onions, carrots and parsnips, and continue cooking until they are tender. Meanwhile, make a dumpling dough with $\frac{1}{2}$ lb (plain) flour, a teaspoon of baking powder and one of salt, 3 oz good fresh beef suet, finely grated, and water to mix to a stiff dough.

Remove the meat and vegetables, and put them on a hot dish in a warm place. Bring the liquid back to boil, roll the dumpling mixture into balls, and drop in the pan. Cook them for about 12 to 15 minutes, depending on their size. Take out the dumplings when they are done, and arrange them on the dish with the meat. Serve with mustard sauce, or onion sauce, Pease Pudding and big, floury, boiled potatoes. The cooking liquor serves as a gravy. Serves 6–8.

# Cottage Pie

1 *lb lean minced beef*
*a large onion*
*a carrot or two*
1 *lb potatoes*

*flour and butter*
*milk, salt and pepper*
*beef dripping*
*a little stock or Oxo*

Slice the onion and fry it in dripping until soft but not brown. Fry also the carrots, scraped and sliced. Add the mince, a tablespoon of flour, salt and pepper. Fry until the meat loses its raw appearance, then add the stock – about a teacupful – and simmer gently, for 20–30 minutes. Meanwhile, peel and quarter the potatoes, put them in cold water and boil until they are soft. Mash them very well, so that there are no lumps whatever. Add a good piece of butter, about 1–2 oz, and enough milk to make a soft mash. Season well with salt and pepper and taste. Put the meat in a pie dish, cover with the mashed potato, and fluff the surface with a fork. Dot all over with butter, and place in an oven at 375°, for 30 minutes. Turn up the heat to 425° or 450° to brown, or brown under a hot grill. Serves 4.

# Boiled Gammon and Parsley Sauce

*a fine joint of gammon*
*breadcrumbs*

*Parsley Sauce*

Soak the gammon overnight in cold water. Put in a large pan, cover with fresh water and bring to the boil. Lower the heat to simmering point and cook for 4 hours, or calculate 20 minutes per lb. The gammon should be left in the water for a good 30 minutes after it has cooked, so add this time to your calculations. To serve, remove the skin and trim the fat neatly. Coat with golden, baked or toasted breadcrumbs, and place a frill on the bone. Serve with Parsley Sauce (see page 31), Pease Pudding, mustard, broad beans.

# Lancashire Hot Pot

Charles Dickens noted that 'oysters and poverty seem to go together', for they were once plentiful, and were an ingredient in Lancashire Hot Pot. The meat used would have been the long boned chops of the middle neck of mutton, and the scrag end; onions and potatoes completed the dish. Mrs Bridges' recipe gives 'scrag end neck of mutton', but omits the oysters – perhaps they had become too expensive by the turn of the century.

| | |
|---|---|
| 2 *lb lamb or mutton chops* | *dripping* |
| *from the neck* | *parsley and thyme* |
| 3 *lamb's kidneys* | *flour* |
| *a large onion* | *salt and pepper* |
| 1½ *lb potatoes* | *pint of stock, or water and Oxo* |

Trim the chops, taking off excess fat. Flour and season them. Slice the onion and the kidneys. Peel the potatoes and cut them into slices (about ¼ inch thick). Fry the chops until nicely browned. Pour the fat into a tall earthenware pot or casserole, and arrange a layer of sliced potatoes at the bottom. Stand the chops upright in the pot (or lay them overlapping in a shallow casserole) and add the onion and kidneys. Season lightly with salt and pepper. Sprinkle chopped parsley over, and add a sprig of thyme to the pot. Fill with layers of potatoes, and pour in the stock. The top of the pot should have a layer of potatoes overlapping. Cover, and cook in a slow oven, about 325° for 2½–3 hours. Remove the lid from the pot during the last 30 minutes, and increase the heat to brown the potatoes. The traditional accompaniment to hot pot is pickled red cabbage. Serves 4–6.

# Irish Stew

Another recipe using scrag or mutton chops. The flavour of Irish stew is much improved by using mutton instead of lamb; onions increase the flavour and potatoes add bulk, but carrots or turnips, for some reason, are never included.

| | |
|---|---|
| 2 *lb neck of mutton* | *parsley and thyme* |
| 2 *lb potatoes* | *salt and pepper* |
| 1 *lb onions* | |

Trim excess fat from the meat. Peel and slice the onions and potatoes. Use a thick-bottomed stewpan or casserole with a close-fitting lid. Put a layer of meat in the pan, season with salt and pepper. Add a layer of onions and one of potatoes, another layer of meat, and so on, ending with a layer of potatoes. Lightly season each layer, and sprinkle with finely chopped parsley, and thyme. Add a little water or stock, ¾ pint should be sufficient, but take care to moisten the top potatoes. Cover securely, and simmer for 3 hours, without removing the lid – be sure that the stew simmers but does not boil. Serve with boiled cabbage, well peppered. Serves 4–6.

# Braised Oxtail and Parsnips

2 lb oxtail, cut in pieces
4 medium size parsnips
an onion, a carrot and a
   turnip
sprig of thyme

dripping
flour
salt and pepper
stock

Some oxtails require previous soaking in salt water, especially those long-frozen. Ask your butcher whether you will need to pre-soak the meat, and if so, leave it overnight – the longer the better. Slice the onion and carrot, cut the turnip in small squares. Fry them gently in dripping until faintly brown. Add the oxtail, well floured and seasoned, and more fat if needed. Fry until brown. Scrape and quarter the parsnips. Put all the vegetables and meat in a casserole, add the thyme and cover with stock or water. Put the lid on the casserole, and cook in an oven at 350° for 2 hours, or until the meat is tender. At the point of sending the dish to the table, the meat should be just about to fall from the bone. Serves 4.

# Steak and Kidney Pie

'Too many cooks spoil the broth of this dish,' wrote Mrs Bridges archly, 'by frying the meat first. It deprives the pie of its good, strong gravy.'

2 lb lean beef steak, chuck,
   flank or skirt
2 or 3 calves' kidneys
8 oz puff or shortcrust pastry
flour
stock or water
mixed herbs

teaspoonful of Lea & Perrins'
   Worcestershire Sauce
salt, pepper
mushrooms (optional) (not
   included in Mrs Bridges'
   recipe)
egg and milk

Trim and cut the meat into cubes, slice the kidneys, flour and season well. Put the meat in a pie dish and sprinkle with herbs, add mushrooms if desired.

Cover with water or stock, add a teaspoonful of Worcestershire Sauce. Cover the pie dish with a nice pastry, decorate with pastry leaves and brush with a wash of beaten egg yolk and milk. Put the pie in a hot oven, 450° for 30 minutes, or until the pastry is well risen and brown. Cover with a piece of greaseproof paper or foil, turn the oven down to 350°, and cook a further 2 hours.

An alternative method of preparing this pie is to stew the meat first, in a stewpan, until tender. The meat is left to get cool, and then covered with the pastry. There are two advantages to this method: one is that the pastry has less cooking, and is therefore lighter, the other is that there will be more gravy, since the cook can add more stock to the pan, and regulate the quantity. Half the gravy is put in the pie dish with the meat, the other half reserved in the pan to be served with the pie. Serves 4–6.

## Steak and Kidney Pudding

This was Mrs Harcourt's original, Sussex recipe, for Sussex is the home of the meat suet pudding. The suet is all important in producing a fine, rich crust. Beef kidney suet should be used, in the proportions of $\frac{3}{4}$ lb suet to each pound of flour. The suet must be very finely chopped or grated, with no lumps. Rub the suet well into the flour, add a teaspoon of salt, and enough water to make a smooth paste. The paste should line the basin about $\frac{1}{4}$ inch thick. The pudding deserves and repays long cooking, at least 6 hours, claims Mrs Harcourt, but 8 hours for preference.

*2 lb beef steak*
*½ lb ox kidney*
*flour*
*2 medium onions*
*parsley and thyme*

*suet pastry made with 1 lb*
*  flour*
*stock or water*
*salt and pepper*

Cut the meat into cubes, roughly chop the kidney, roll in seasoned flour. Skin and slice the onions. Roll out the suet crust and line a 3-pint basin, but be careful not to stretch it. Trim off the pastry around the rim of the basin. Fill the basin with chopped onions and meat, adding finely chopped parsley and thyme, lightly season, and pour in enough stock or water, and fill to within an inch of the top. Cut a circle in the remaining paste to fit the top, moisten the edges and seal well.

Cover the paste with greased and floured paper, then with a damp pudding cloth, also well floured. Tie under the rim of the basin, bring the corners up to the centre and tie in a knot. Lower the basin on a trivet into a large pan of gently boiling water, cover with a lid, and boil for 8 hours, adding more boiling water from the kettle when needed. Always serve the pudding from the basin, it is never done to invert and unmould. Serves 4–6.

# Toad-in-the-Hole

'I have never understood the reason for the name of this dish,' wrote Mrs Bridges, 'having never seen a toad in a hole. Nasty, fat, warty things. I make *my* toad with lean beef leftovers.' In her day, Toad-in-the-Hole was usually made with leftover meat, all manner of things going into the batter, but today it is usual to stick to sausages.

2 *eggs*
4 *oz plain flour*
1 *lb pork or beef sausages*

1 *teaspoon salt*
$\frac{3}{8}$ *pint milk*

Sift the flour and salt into a mixing bowl, make a well in the centre, and break the eggs into it. Add half the milk, and stir into the flour. Add the rest of the milk by degrees, keeping the mixture free from lumps until you have a smooth batter. Fry the sausages until they are light brown, and transfer them to a 10-inch baking dish 2 inches deep. Pour the batter over them and put the dish in an oven set at 400°. Bake for 30 minutes, or until the batter has risen well, crisp and brown. Serves 4.

# Raised Pork Pie

(to make 2 pies each weighing 1½ lb)

2 *lb pork, not too lean – a quarter fat to threequarters lean*
*nutmeg, salt, paprika, sage*

*aspic jelly*
1 *lb of hot water crust (page 158)*
*egg and milk*

Mince the pork quite finely, and add a teaspoon of salt, one of paprika, a little grated nutmeg and a pinch of dried sage. Take the warm pastry and divide in half. Keep one half in a warm place. Reserve a quantity for the lid of the pie, roll the rest into a ball. Grease the bottom of a milk bottle and flour it. Press it into the ball of dough, and start bringing up the paste with your hands, turning the bottle and 'raising' the paste. Try and achieve a regular and fairly thin crust. Remove the bottle when the paste has cooled. Make a lid by pressing out the reserved piece, fill the pie with the minced pork.

Moisten the edges of the paste, lay the lid on and pinch the edges together to seal: this is best done with the left forefinger and the right forefinger and thumb. Make a hole in the top of each pie, and brush with egg and milk wash, or a wash made with a thick solution of Marmite mixed with beaten egg yolk. Repeat the process with the rest of the pastry and the minced pork. Place the pies in an oven set at 300° for 1½ hours. When they have cooked, allow them to cool for an hour before pouring aspic jelly into the holes.

# Brawn

There were three recipes for brawn in the original book, one made with a whole pig's head, another with pig's cheek and this one, made with beef and trotters:

6 *trotters*
1 *lb lean shin of beef*
4 *teaspoons salt*

2 *medium onions*
4 *crushed cloves*
*pepper*

Put the trotters and the beef in a stewpan, and cover with water to the depth of about 1 inch. Add half the salt. Bring to the boil and skim until the scum no longer rises to the surface. Now add the onions, coarsely chopped, and the crushed cloves, and simmer for 2 hours or until the meat is tender. Transfer the meat and trotters to a dish, and strain the cooking liquid through a fine sieve. Remove the skin and bones from the trotters, chop them and the meat coarsely. Add ½ pint of the strained liquid, the rest of the salt, and some pepper, and pour into a brawn mould, and leave until firmly set.

# Pig's Trotters

6 *trotters*
2 *onions*
2 *carrots*
*parsley, bay leaf and thyme*

*salt and pepper, a blade of
mace*
1½ *pints stock*

Split the trotters, then bind them in their original shape. Put them with the sliced onions and carrots into a stewpan, cover with stock, bring to the boil and skim. Add the parsley, bay leaf and thyme, tied in a bunch, the blade of mace, salt and pepper. Boil for 2 hours. The trotters may be eaten hot, in which case thicken some of the cooking liquor with flour, and add some finely chopped parsley. Serve with Pease Pudding and turnip tops. To be eaten cold, leave them until the jelly sets, and serve with oil and vinegar and chopped capers.


# Tripe and Onions

There used to be special tripe butchers at one time, who sold tripe and onions ready cooked, or dressed tripe for cooking. It was a much loved Cockney dish in gaslight London.

| | |
|---|---|
| 2 lb dressed tripe | 2 heaped tablespoons flour |
| 6 onions | parsley |
| 2 pints milk | salt and pepper |
| 2 oz butter | |

Cut the tripe into small squares and slice the onions. Put them in the stewpan, add the milk, and simmer until the tripe is nice and tender – it can take 1–1½ hours. Make a roux with the flour and butter and add the milk by degrees, blending until smooth. Add finely chopped parsley, and pour over the tripe and onions in a serving dish. Serves 4–6.


# Devilled Beef Bones

These bones were leftovers from 'upstairs' roast ribs of beef, and much enjoyed as a supper dish by the kitchen staff, spread with seasoned butter and grilled. The ribs may be uncooked and seasoned. Mix 3 oz butter with 2 teaspoons of Lea & Perrins' Worcestershire Sauce, 1 teaspoon of mustard, black pepper, cayenne pepper and salt. Spread on the scored ribs, and put in a hot oven, 425° for 10–15 minutes. Otherwise, if the ribs are cold leftovers, spread with the butter and brown under the grill.


# Steak and Onions

Another leftovers dish, where slices of cooked beef were fried with onions and covered in warmed gravy, a practice of which Mrs Bridges strongly disapproved. 'Steak and onions is a fried dish, and quick to prepare, it is also economical. [Rump steak was around 1s 3d lb, and one of the most expensive cuts of beef, so what did she mean by 'economical'?] Some households object to the smell of frying onions.'

The dish should not be too fatty. Trim the fat from some raw rump steak. Serve one medium-size onion to every half pound of steak. Skin the onion and slice it in rings, and fry in a little beef dripping, until they are golden – it is a good idea to sprinkle a tiny amount of caster sugar over the frying onions (it makes them browner and crisper). Put the onions on a serving dish, and fry the meat until tender, about ten minutes. Swill the frying pan with stock or water, add a nut of butter and pour over the steak.

# Stuffed Shoulder of Lamb or Mutton

*a 2 lb shoulder of lamb*　　　　*bouquet garni*
*a carrot, an onion and a*　　　　*1 stock cube*
　*small turnip*　　　　　　　　*1 oz each flour and butter*

For the stuffing:

*1 oz butter*　　　　　　　*4 oz breadcrumbs*
*4 oz mushrooms*　　　　　*salt and pepper*
*an onion*　　　　　　　　*mixed herbs*
*2 slices cooked ham*　　　*gravy or stock*

Bone the shoulder with a sharp knife, taking care not to pierce the skin. Put the bone in a saucepan with a sliced onion, carrot and turnip, the *bouquet garni* and the Oxo cube. Cover with water, bring to the boil, skim and simmer for at least 1 hour. Make a stuffing by slicing the onion and mushrooms finely, and sautéing them in butter. Cut up the ham equally finely, add a pinch of mixed dried herbs, season with salt and pepper, add the breadcrumbs. Mix all the ingredients together, and sufficient stock (taken from the simmering bone and veg) to make a stuffing paste. Stuff the shoulder of lamb, and sew up the edges with thread or string. This is essential, otherwise the meat will open up and the stuffing will fall out. Roast at 375° and give 25–30 minutes per lb, the meat weighed after having been stuffed. Make a brown roux with the butter and flour, and add the stock by degrees until smooth. When the roast has cooked, pour off excess fat from the roasting tin, and add any juices and browned sediments to the sauce. Serve with the meat, sliced and arranged on a hot serving dish. Serves 6.

# VEGETABLES

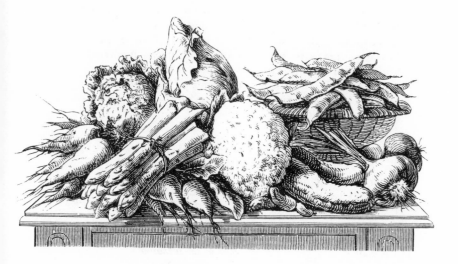

Although Mrs Bridges acknowledges the French practice of serving certain vegetables as a separate course, she was bound to the British habit of including vegetables with the meat. Nothing so delights the English eye as a plate of roast meat abetted by roast potatoes, peas, carrots, cauliflower and the like. However, Mrs Bridges had no intention of giving in without a fight, and this is what she wrote in her Introduction to the Vegetable chapter: 'No dinner can be thought a success unless the vegetables receive the due care and consideration which should be accorded to them ... whenever the vegetables are distinguished for their excellence, the dinner is always particularly enjoyed. The delicacy of a dish of fine vegetables always ensures it a good reception when properly prepared. This is particularly so in France, where the dish of some vegetable at the end of the dinner is as eagerly anticipated as a pudding or tart at an English table. But in many houses in England one only sees those vegetables which accompany the meat to make a pile of confusion upon the plate. It is an English habit to look upon vegetables as a "dish of herbs" as food only fit for peasants who are incapable of appreciating a dish in its own right. The arti-

114

choke and asparagus are the only examples of vegetables taken separately in England, and this only because they cannot be attacked with a knife and fork.'

In her reference to a 'dish of herbs', Mrs Bridges touched on a deeply-rooted theory that vegetables were mainly medicinal. Even in the 1930s a popular cookery book listed the dietary properties of vegetables; carrots were good for asthma, celery acts on the nervous system, spinach has a direct effect on the kidneys, and watercress is good for scurvy and anaemia. It took the potato two hundred years to become reluctantly accepted from the time of its introduction in the 16th century; what had originally accompanied meat was not potatoes, but bread and, of course, ale. In Mrs Bridges' day there were not a few people who were puzzled as to the true role of the tomato – was it fruit or vegetable, and how should it best be treated? Today, she would be astonished at the wide variety available, vegetables relatively unknown at the turn of this century – courgettes, eggplant, avocado pears, corn on the cob and fennel, and the familiar ones in quantity and quality to be had the year round. Mrs Bridges would be impressed by the absence of insects. In her book she writes, 'Give vegetables a sharp tap before you wash them, and the dirt, sand and insects will drop off, which would otherwise stick when put into water. Add vinegar to the water as it draws out the caterpillars.' She goes on to advise cooks on how to prevent cabbage and onions from 'creating a disagreeable odour throughout the house.' Put a piece of bread wrapped in muslin in the pan, and keep some vinegar and water boiling on the stove while vegetables are being cooked. All green vegetables should be cooked in rapidly boiling water, and never overcooked so that they become soft and mushy, and always boil with the lid off. Root vegetables should be put into cold water before cooking, while leaf vegetables and all those that grow above the soil should be plunged into fast-boiling water. Never serve fried vegetables in a dish with a lid on – they will quickly go limp and soggy Always try to improve the appearance of vegetables by glazing with butter or a little meat glaze. Sprinkle them with finely chopped herbs – parsley, mint, tarragon and savory. Never over-butter or over-sauce a dish, too much spoils both the appearance and the taste.

With few exceptions, Mrs Bridges' recipes are fairly simple and straightforward. Her book included no recipes for tomatoes, none for courgettes or 'modern' vegetables, and we have not included any from other sources. She might not have approved, and this is, after all, her book.

# VEGETABLES

## The Upstairs Recipes

Chou Rouge à
    l'Alsacienne
Chou Rouge à la
    Flamande
Chou Farci
Carottes Vichy
Endives Braisées
Petits pois à la
    Française
Pommes Anna
Pommes Duchesse
Pommes de Terre
    Dauphine
Gratin Dauphinois
Pommes de Terre
    Pont-Neuf
Pommes de Terre
    Soufflées

# Chou Rouge à l'Alsacienne

There are but few recipes for cabbage in the repertoire; green
cabbage is usually stuffed or braised, while red cabbage is
cooked with apples or chestnuts. These last mentioned dishes
were brought from provincial obscurity and introduced into the
repertoire by Escoffier. Mrs Bridges' book must have been one of
the first English language cookery books to include these recipes.

*1 red cabbage*
*pork dripping*
*4 oz bacon*

*½ pint white stock*
*½ lb chestnuts*

Shred the cabbage finely, and fry it for a few minutes in an
ounce of pork dripping. Cut the bacon in dice, mix in with the
cabbage, and moisten with the stock. The dish should be cooked
in a covered casserole in the oven. Boil the chestnuts for 10
minutes, drain, and peel them while hot with a sharp knife.
Holding the chestnuts in a cloth makes this operation less pain-
ful. Split the nuts in two, and mix them in with the cabbage.
Season with salt, black pepper, and cook in a slow oven, 300–325°
for 1½ hours. Serves 4–6.

# Chou Rouge à la Flamande

*1 red cabbage*
*1 onion*
*pork dripping*
*4 pippin or russet apples*

*vinegar*
*1 dessertspoonful sugar*
*salt, pepper, nutmeg*

Slice the onion, and cook until soft in an ounce of pork dripping.
Slice the cabbage finely, and sauté it in the fat with the onion.
Put into a cocotte or casserole, well buttered. Season with salt,
pepper and a little grated nutmeg, and moisten with a dessertspoon of wine vinegar. Cook in an oven at 325° for 1 hour, then
add the peeled and sliced apples, and a sprinkling of sugar. Cover
again, and cook for a further hour. Serves 4–6.

# Chou Farci

savoy cabbage
1 onion
4 oz sausage meat
4 rashers streaky bacon
2 oz cooked peas
6 tablespoons cooked rice

4 tomatoes
half clove of garlic
$\frac{1}{2}$ teaspoon mixed dried herbs
salt, black pepper
pork dripping

Slice the onion and chop up the bacon, and cook in pork dripping until the onions are soft. Cut a cavity in the heart of the cabbage, about $2\frac{1}{2}$–3 inches across, large enough to receive the stuffing. Have a large pan of boiling water, and plunge the cabbage into it for three minutes, remove and plunge into cold water. Put the tomatoes in the pan for a moment or two – the boiling water makes them easier to skin. Fry the sausage meat, add the garlic finely minced, the mixed herbs, salt and pepper. Chop the tomatoes and add them to the sausage mixture, also add the rice and peas and the finely chopped heart of the cabbage. Cook gently for a further 5 minutes, taste for seasoning. Drain the cabbage thoroughly, and stuff the centre with some of the mixture. Then spread the mixture well between the leaves, working outwards until all of the mixture is used up. Wrap the cabbage in muslin or fine cloth, place in a casserole with a lid, and add a half pint of water. Cook in an oven set at 300° for $2$–$2\frac{1}{2}$ hours. Very carefully, remove the cabbage from the cloth, the best way to do this is to invert the cabbage, placing a close-fitting collander, sieve or shallow bowl on the cabbage, then take away the cloth. Turn the cabbage on to a serving dish, taking care to retain its shape. Serves 4.

# Carottes Vichy

1 lb young carrots
1 oz butter to glaze

1 tablespoon cream
chopped parsley

The carrots may be cooked whole, or scraped and sliced. Cook them in boiling, salted water until tender, then drain. Sauté for a minute or two in butter and sprinkle with sugar, in order to glaze them. Add a tablespoon of cream and sprinkle with chopped parsley before serving. Serves 4.

# Endives Braisées

8 *endives*
*juice of ½ lemon*
*2 oz butter*
*¼ pint water (approx)*

*salt*
*Espagnole sauce or fonds lié*
*chopped parsley*

Wash the endives thoroughly. Put them in a casserole with the water, butter, a pinch of salt and the lemon juice, sufficient to barely cover them. Cut a piece of greaseproof paper to fit the pan, butter it well, and place it on top of the endives. Simmer over a very low heat until they are tender – about 30 minutes. Drain them of all the liquid, and glaze them for a minute or two in warm butter. Before serving, pour a few spoonfuls of sauce or *demi-glace* over them, and a sprinkling of chopped parsley. Serves 4.

# Petit pois à la Française

1 *lb shelled young peas*
4 *slices streaky bacon*
1 *medium onion*

1 *teaspoon sugar*
1 *lettuce heart, shredded*
*salt and pepper*

Slice the onion finely, chop the bacon, and sauté together in a little butter until the onions are soft, but do not allow them to brown. Add the peas, sprinkle with sugar and season with salt and pepper. Add just enough water to cover the peas, and simmer gently until they are tender. Add the lettuce heart and let it cook for a few minutes until it goes soft. Ideally, the water should almost evaporate by the time the peas are cooked; the lettuce softens in the heat of the peas. Sometimes, tiny pickling onions, previously cooked in water, are added to this dish. Serves 4–6.

# Pommes de Terre Anna

A potato cake of thinly sliced potatoes, cooked golden brown. Peel and thinly slice some potatoes. Season, and lay the slices in a sauté pan or shallow Pyrex dish, well buttered. Add another layer of slices, lightly seasoned and well buttered, and continue filling the dish. Bake at 375–400° until they are browning on the underside, about 30 minutes, then turn the cake over and give them another 10 minutes.

## Pommes de Terre Duchesse

Fried potato shapes or croquettes. Make a purée of boiled potatoes.
Mash the potatoes with butter, but do not make them too soft and light. Season well with salt and pepper. To every pound of potatoes add 2 egg yolks; this will produce a workable paste. Shape as desired, and dust with flour before frying the shapes in butter.

## Pommes de Terre Dauphine

To make these deep-fried, cork-shaped potato cakes, take 8 oz of the previous recipe for Duchesse potatoes. Blend it thoroughly with 2 oz unsweetened Choux paste (see recipe on page 162) flavoured with a little grated nutmeg. When the mixture is cool enough to handle, shape into corks, flour, dip in beaten egg and fine breadcrumbs. Fry in deep fat. Salt lightly before serving. Serves 4–6.

## Gratin Dauphinois

Sliced potatoes cooked in milk and cheese in the oven.
Peel and slice some potatoes and par-boil them in milk; they should be sliced about $\frac{1}{8}$-inch thick. Put a layer in a sauté pan, or shallow braising dish, well buttered. Season with salt and pepper, and cover with a thin layer of grated Gruyère cheese. Continue in layers of seasoned potatoes and cheese until the dish is filled. Pour in enough single cream thinned slightly with milk to cover, and set in an oven at 375° until browned.

# Pommes de Terre Pont-Neuf

Square-cut chipped potatoes, the traditional accompaniment to Tournedos Henry IV. The chips are served like building-bricks, arranged in crossed, three-tiered layers.

Peel some potatoes, and slice them into lengths of finger-thickness. Square off the ends, and fry them in deep fat. Just before serving, fry again in very hot fat to give a crisp crust. Drain and dredge lightly with salt.

# Pommes de Terre Soufflées

Puffed up, golden potato cushions. They are not always easy to achieve, since there is a matter of chance in the cooking of them. One should have a fat thermometer to get good results. Nowadays it is possible to purchase an electric deep fryer which can always produce a high proportion of perfect Pommes Soufflées. Correct temperatures are the trick. Choose good quality potatoes, and cut them in ovals or cushion shapes, about $\frac{3}{8}$ inch thick. Allow the fat or oil to reach a temperature of 325°. Dry the slices, and lower them into the fat. Turn them occasionally with a spoon so that they cook evenly, and give them 5–6 minutes. Take them from the fat, and increase the temperature to 400°. Plunge the slices into the fat, and they will puff up into cushions, theoretically. Various recipes give widely varying temperatures, but 375° and 400° give good results, bearing in mind that the type of potato can vary considerably.

# VEGETABLES

## The Downstairs Recipes

Braised Onions
Stuffed Onions
Stuffed Vegetable
   Marrow
Pease Pudding
Potatoes, Mashed,
   Baked, Roasted
   and Fried
Carrots and Swedes
Cauliflower Cheese
Bubble & Squeak
Parsnip Fritters

# Braised Onions

Choose Spanish onions, skin them, and boil in salted water about 1 hour. Drain, and place them in an ovenproof dish with a lid. Pour bacon fat over them, or butter, season with salt and pepper and sprinkle with sugar. Cover, and bake at 325° for a further hour, or until tender. They may be served as they are, or with a little good gravy poured over them.

# Stuffed Onions

| | |
|---|---|
| 8 *Spanish onions* | *parsley* |
| ½ *lb minced veal* | *butter* |
| 4 *oz breadcrumbs* | 1 *egg* |
| 4 *oz mushrooms* | *salt, black pepper* |

Par-boil the onions as in the previous recipe, but for a half hour. Drain, and plunge into cold water. Scoop out the inside of each onion, enough to receive a good spoonful of stuffing. Chop the scooped-out part and fry until light brown in butter, with the mushrooms, finely sliced. Mix with the veal, breadcrumbs and chopped parsley. Season with salt and quite a lot of pepper, the stuffing should be highly seasoned. Bind with the egg, and spoon the stuffing into each onion. Put them in a closed pot with enough stock or water to come quarter way up the onions, and braise in an oven set at 325°, until they are tender, about one hour. Serves 4–6.

# Stuffed Vegetable Marrow

Avoid those big, heavy marrows, whose main content is water. Peel a young, medium-size one, and cut it into rings about 1½ inches deep. Remove the centre core of seeds, and sprinkle with coarse salt. Leave for 15 minutes, and rinse. Arrange the pieces in a shallow baking dish and fill the cavities with a mixture of cooked rice, minced veal or beef, a sprinkling of mixed dried herbs, salt and plenty of pepper. The stuffing may be pre-cooked, having sautéed a finely chopped onion in butter, adding the minced meat, herbs, seasoning and rice. Add also a teaspoon tomato purée, and a little stock or water to moisten. Fill the cavities, dot with butter, and bake in a moderate oven, 350°. Sprinkle with a mixture of chopped parsley and breadcrumbs, and brown under the grill before serving. Serves 4–6.

# Pease Pudding

Once a pudding of peas, expedience and poverty, which one could buy from the baker or local cookshop. It is now the traditional accompaniment to boiled beef and carrots or boiled bacon. Soak 1 lb of dried split peas overnight. Boil until tender in salted water, and press through a sieve, or purée in a blender.

Add 2–3 oz butter, and season well with salt and pepper. A richer pudding contains 2 beaten eggs. Mrs Bridges cooked it in the real old-fashioned way, putting the purée in a floured cloth, tying it in a ball and simmering in water for a half hour. Otherwise, put the purée in a buttered pudding basin, cover and steam for half to three-quarters of an hour. Serves 6–8.

# Potatoes

Mrs Bridges laments at some length the general lack of care taken when cooking potatoes. One of the commonest faults, she observes, is cooking them in fast boiling water until they split, neglecting to drain them, and allowing them to become water-logged. 'Potatoes boiled rapidly take just as long to cook as those gently simmered. When boiling potatoes, choose those as near in size as possible. The larger the potato, the slower the boil. When possible or convenient, boil them with the skins on, preserving the rich salts found thereunder. New potatoes soaked in salty water will skin more easily, or shake them up in a bag with coarse sea-salt. Mashed potatoes should be light as a cloud, and fluffy. Make certain that the purée is free of lumps, use plenty of butter, and always *hot* milk. Season with salt and pepper, whisk with a balloon whisk as for egg whites, but do not let them get too cool. To bake large potatoes, prick them all over with a sharp knife or fork, or rub them with lard. Medium size ones take an hour to bake. Split them open and serve with salty butter and finely chopped chives or parsley. Dust chipped potatoes with flour before you fry them, this makes them crisper and browner, and this is especially true of cooked, sliced potatoes which are to be fried. It is permissible to par-boil potatoes before they are roasted, in that it saves time. However, par-boiling renders the outside of the potato rather floury, which thus does not respond so well to basting. Score raw potatoes with a knife before roasting, and baste frequently.'

# Carrots and Swedes

A nice country dish to go with roast meat, and particularly good with fresh young vegetables, but it is also a way of using large, old carrots and swedes. Boil them until tender, drain them in a collander, and chop to fine dice with a sharp knife. Dress with melted butter, and season with lots of salt and white pepper.


# Cauliflower Cheese

*firm, white cauliflower*
*½ pint Béchamel*
*1 oz cheddar cheese*

*1 tablespoonful finely grated*
   *Parmesan*
*salt and cayenne pepper*
*nutmeg*

Remove the tough outer leaves of the cauliflower, cut a cross in the base of the stalk with a sharp knife, and plunge the cauliflower into boiling, salted water. Prepare the Béchamel according to the recipe on page 16, but using 1 oz each butter and flour to a ½ pint of milk. Grate the cheddar and add to the sauce with the Parmesan. Season with salt and cayenne pepper. Test to see if the cauliflower is cooked – it should be slightly firm – a cauliflower undercooked is far preferable to one that is overcooked and waterlogged. Drain the cauliflower thoroughly, put it into a heat-proof dish, pour the sauce over, and brown it under the grill or in a very hot oven. Scrape a little nutmeg on top before serving. Before saucing the cauliflower, mop up any excess water that has drained from it with kitchen paper. Serves 4.


# Bubble & Squeak

Mrs Bridges' recipe calls for cold, cooked beef or mutton, fried with greens. In the past seventy years, Bubble and Squeak has developed into a cake of fried, mashed potato and cabbage or, more commonly, cooked Brussels sprouts. Whatever the combination, the most important thing is to fry to a crisp brown, mash with a fork, turn the cake over, fry and mash, and so on until the crispy bits are well incorporated into the whole. Finish by frying the cake both sides until a deep, crisp brown.

## Parsnip Fritters

3 *medium size parsnips*
3 *tablespoons plain flour*
1 *tablespoon olive oil*

1 *egg white*
*pinch of bicarbonate of soda*
*salt and pepper*

Scrape the parsnips, halve and quarter them, cut the quarters into pieces 1–1½ inches long. Boil in salted water until tender. Meanwhile, make the batter. Put the flour into a bowl with a pinch of salt. Add the oil, and mix. Now add warm water to make a batter like thick cream. When the parsnips are cooked, drain them, dry on paper towels, and season with salt. Beat an egg white stiff, until it forms peaks. Add a pinch of bicarbonate of soda to the batter, and beat in a spoonful of the egg white. Now fold in the rest of the white, and drop the parsnip pieces in the batter; see that they are well coated. Deep fry in smoking hot oil, until they are well puffed up and golden. Dredge with salt, and serve on a napkin. Serves 4–6.

# DESSERTS, PUDDINGS & SAVOURIES

Mrs Bridges lived in the age of puddings – steamed, boiled and baked, which is why she included one hundred and sixty of these solid, British rib-stickers in her book. Five years later, in 1910, Cassell's *Shilling Cookery* responded to public demand and gave recipes for three hundred and seventy, 'the greatest number of recipes ever given in any cookery book yet published'. Very few of these puddings possessed the finesse of a soufflé, or a bavaroise, for they were designed to quell the appetites of large Victorian families. From the basic ingredients of flour, breadcrumbs, suet, sugar and eggs, endless permutations were possible and indeed expected, for this was also the age of invention. It saw the introduction of photography, batteries, the safety pin and the motor car. Mrs Bridges probably benefited from the invention of the refrigerator and the gas cooker, while Hudson the butler got a smoother shave from the new safety razor.

How could cooks resist the challenge? From Victorian farmhouses and city kitchens came a pudding for each day of the year: Adelaide and Albert, College and Cabinet, Railway and Military, Newmarket, Monmouth, Paradise and Porcupine – with a further three hundred and fifty-five to come! They even invented a pudding to commemorate the annexing of Ashanti, on the Gold Coast, in 1901, and in the Royal Military Academy cadets enjoyed a sponge pudding shot full of sultanas, which celebrated the battle of the Alma in the Crimea.

Faced with such competition, how did the fashionable confections of Paris become established on British menus? Escoffier, working at the Carlton Hotel, invented the Peach Melba which, like its close associate *Poires Belle Hélène*, has been more variously (and badly) interpreted than practically any other dessert in the repertoire. It is unlikely that Mrs Bridges had heard of Peach Melba, and she omits the recipe in her book. Instead, she includes several of the latest fancies introduced from the Continental resorts – *Goronflot à la Cannes*, and *Cake à la Trouville*. Who makes them today? They were then as fashionable and impermanent as an Easter bonnet, and have not withstood the test of time as have Chocolate Mousse and Crêpes Suzette.

Many of the puddings selected for the *Upstairs, Downstairs Cookery Book* would be equally appreciated in either domain, and are common to both. Christmas Pudding, for example, and Gooseberry Fool, Apple Pie and Apple Charlotte, Summer Pudding and Trifle. But there is no doubt as to where Tea Soufflé belongs, and perhaps Mrs Bridges prepared it for the French Ambassador when he dined at Eaton Place, as a spoonful of *entente cordiale*. Champagne Sorbet, too, is decidedly 'upstairs', for it featured on the menu when King Edward VII came to dine, and it demanded a long and tiresome preparation, turning the handle of the ice-machine.

Few cooks bother to make their own ices today, preferring to buy the many excellent commercial varieties available. Puddings in tins, or frozen in packets, however, cannot really compete with a true British pudding, boiled for six hours in a cloth, and served to an audience dumb with admiration. Cooks don't cook for themselves, they cook for others, producing as a fitting climax a pudding wreathed in cream, or coated with custard, or decorated with holly and ignited with brandy. Whatever disasters might have gone before are now forgotten. Which is why puddings were invented. Savouries appear only to have been really established at the beginning of this century, and they originated from the cheese course which formed an important role as an aid to digestion. They were supposed to add piquancy to the end of the meal, and to offset the sweetness of the dessert. They were all very 'upstairs'. Several of these dishes became well established outside the dining-room, and formed the foundation of the great British 'snack' – Welsh rarebit, roes on toast, sardines on toast. Had the savoury failed to become established, we might have been deprived of those two great creations, a gap which no imagination could otherwise fill – baked beans and spaghetti on toast. They would have gone down a treat in Eaton Place.

# DESSERTS

## The Upstairs Recipes

Apricots Colbert
Champagne Sorbet
Charlotte Malakoff
Christmas Pudding
Gooseberry Fool
Nesselrode and
   Clermont Bavarois
Queen of Puddings
Réligieuse
Tea Soufflé
Summer Pudding
Syllabub
Tarte aux Framboises

# Apricots Colbert

12 *whole apricots (a large tin*     1 *egg yolk*
    *of apricots may be used)*      *vanilla essence*
3 *oz rice*                           *or sugar*
½ *pint water*                1 *whole egg*
3 *tablespoons sugar*       *breadcrumbs*

Blanch the rice by boiling for a minute or two, then rinse in cold
water. Make a thin sugar syrup with the water and 2 tablespoons of sugar, and add the rice. Cook until the water is
absorbed or the rice is tender. Allow to cool, then stir in the egg
yolk. Halve the apricots, remove the stones, and poach them in
water with vanilla sugar or essence, add a tablespoon of sugar,
and cook until they are tender (or use tinned halves of apricots).
When they are cool, sandwich together with spoonfuls of the
rice – a dessertspoon per apricot is about right. Put them in the
refrigerator to chill for 30 minutes. Beat the whole egg, and dip
each apricot, then roll in breadcrumbs. Fry them in deep, hot fat
until light brown and crisp. Serve at once on a white napkin.
Serves 4–6.

# Champagne Sorbet

1 *pint demi-sec Champagne*     *Italian meringue:*
1 *pint water*                   4 *oz loaf sugar*
8 *oz (preferably loaf) sugar*    3–4 *tablespoons water*
*juice of* 2 *lemons and* 1 *orange*    2 *egg whites*

Dissolve the sugar in the water in a saucepan. Take care to stir
it with a wooden spoon by drawing the spoon once or twice across
in one direction. Care must also be taken that there are no grains
of sugar remaining on the sides of the pan, which cause the sugar
to grain and go opaque. Heat gently until the sugar is completely
dissolved, and boil steadily for 7–8 minutes, or until the syrup
registers 15° on a saccharometer. Pour the champagne into a
bowl, add the fruit juices and the syrup and stir thoroughly.
Leave in freezing compartment until firm but not set, and stir.
Now add the Italian meringue, made by boiling the sugar and
water as above, but to 260° on the thermometer, adding the
whipped egg whites to form meringue. If you do not have a sugar
thermometer, use either ordinary meringue, or whipped cream.
The proportions are a quarter of the bulk of the sorbet. Stir the

meringue or the cream into the sorbet, and return to freeze. The mixture when ready should not be solid, but rather light and slushy. Just before serving, add a spoonful of champagne to the sorbet.

# Charlotte Malakoff

Simpler to prepare than the famous Charlotte Russe, but none-the-less rich and creamy. Of all the Charlotte recipes given by Mrs Bridges, this seems to have been the favourite at Eaton Place. Most cold Charlotte recipes call for sponge fingers, which are cheaper and better when made at home.

For the sponge fingers:

2½ oz flour                          3 eggs
2½ oz sugar

Separate the yolks from the whites, and beat the yolks with the sugar until light and creamy. Whip the whites to a stiff froth. Fold in the sifted flour and the whites alternately. If wished, the batter may be flavoured with a little vanilla. Grease a baking sheet, or greaseproof paper, and pour small quantities of batter with a dessertspoon, to form fingers according to the depth of your mould – 3½–4 inches is usual. Sift caster sugar over them, and bake in an oven set at 350° for 15 minutes, until the sponge fingers are light brown. Makes about 25–30 fingers.
Take a 5-inch Charlotte mould, and cut a piece of greaseproof paper to fit the bottom. Boil a heaped tablespoon of sugar with two tablespoons of water until it begins to thicken – about 4 minutes. Trim the edges of the fingers and fit them face outwards around the mould, glueing the joins with the syrup.

For the filling:

4 oz sugar                           4 oz double cream
4 oz ground almonds                  1 glass or miniature bottle
4 oz unsalted butter                    of Kirsch

Cream the butter with the sugar until light and fluffy. Add the ground almonds, the Kirsch and mix thoroughly. Whip the cream until it begins to thicken, but it should not be stiff. Fold into the mixture. Spoon into the Charlotte mould and leave to chill. When firm, trim off the ends of the sponge fingers, and invert the mould onto a serving dish. Remove the disc of paper, and decorate the top with sweetened, vanilla-flavoured whipped cream. A few crystallised violets may be employed. Serves 8–10.

## Christmas Pudding

8 oz flour
4 oz fresh, white breadcrumbs
8 oz Barbados sugar
6 eggs
¼ pint Barley wine or
    Yorkshire Stingo
2 tablespoons brandy
8 oz currants
12 oz seedless raisins
12 oz sultanas
4 oz candied peel

6 oz blanched slivered almonds
8 oz suet
4 oz glacé cherries
1 cooking apple
grated rind of large lemon
grated rind and juice of 2
    oranges
1 teaspoon mixed spice
½ teaspoon cinnamon
½ grated nutmeg
1 teaspoon salt

Finely chop the cherries and the candied peel, put them in a large, deep bowl with the rest of the dried fruit. Peel, slice and chop the apple, add the grated lemon and orange peel and the almonds. Now add the suet, flour, breadcrumbs, sugar and spices and the salt. Mix thoroughly, add the well-beaten eggs, the ale and the brandy and the fruit juice. Stir, wish, and leave overnight.

Put the mixture into pudding basins (there will be enough to fill four 1½-pint basins) and leave an inch or two at the top, for the mixture to swell. Cover with greaseproof paper (or foil), then with a cloth tied below the rim securely with string. Put the puddings in pans, each on a trivet if possible, and with water three-quarters of the way up the basins. Simmer on a very low heat for 8 hours, replenishing with boiling water when necessary. The puddings should be left to mature for a month before Christmas. When you are ready to use them, change the cloth on each basin for a fresh one, put the puddings to boil on a low heat as before, and simmer for two hours. Before taking the puddings to table, warm some brandy in a saucepan, pour over the puddings and set light to it with a taper. Serve with brandy butter or cream. If you are of a mind to do so, wrap some sixpences in paper, and press them into the pudding on the top, before inverting it on to the serving dish.

# Gooseberry Fool

One of the most elegant and simple of English desserts, it should not be made with the addition of gelatine, but simply cream and gooseberry purée.

1 *lb green gooseberries*  
$\frac{3}{4}$ *pint double cream*

3 *heaped tablespoons sugar*

Stew the gooseberries until soft, with the sugar, in as little water as possible. The amount of sugar added depends on the tartness of the fruit. Alternatively, bake the gooseberries in a covered dish, without water, until they are soft. Work them through a sieve to obtain a thick purée, and leave to get cold. Whip the cream until stiff, and gently fold in the purée. Do not bother about blending the two thoroughly, for a marbling effect is quite traditional. Chill for an hour or two before serving. Serve with fine sponge fingers. Serves 6–8.

# Nesselrode and Clermont Puddings

Some confusion seems to exist over these two puddings, and cooks disagree over the exact ingredients. Both are based on the *Crème Bavaroise*, and both involve chestnuts in one form or another. Nesselrode is a *crème* mixed with chestnut purée, and containing dried fruits soaked in liqueur, sometimes served with Apricot Sauce. Clermont is the same thing, but flavoured with rum and omitting the candied fruits. Instead, Clermont contains chopped *marrons glacés* and is decorated with whole marrons. This is Mrs Bridges' recipe, right or wrong.

## Nesselrode or Bavarois

4 oz caster sugar
4 egg yolks
¾ pint milk
¼ oz gelatine
vanilla sugar or essence
Kirsch or maraschino
8 oz double cream

8 oz sweet chestnut purée
  (purée de marrons
  available in tins)
1 teaspoon chopped, candied
  orange peel
1 oz chopped glacé cherries
1 oz sultanas

First, leave the dried fruit to soak in the liqueur. Make a custard, beating the yolks with the sugar until light and creamy, adding the milk just below boiling point, returning to the heat to thicken. Add the vanilla sugar, and stir (preferably over a double boiler) until the mixture coats the back of a spoon. Do not allow it to curdle. Dissolve the gelatine in two tablespoons of hot water (powdered gelatine is easiest to use, and makers' instructions can be followed) and add to the custard. Stir the custard until it has cooled enough to prevent a skin forming, then leave to get cold. Whip the cream until it is firm, but not too stiff, beat the chestnut purée to make it lighter, and fold both into the custard – it should be free of streaks. Pour the custard into an oiled or greased Bavarois mould, or suitable fluted mould of about 1½-pints capacity. When the custard is beginning to firm, add the fruit, drained of any liqueur, and lightly stir it in. Return the mould to chill until set. Serve with Apricot Sauce, made by poaching fresh, stoned apricots in a light sugar syrup until soft. Pass them through a sieve, and add to the syrup. Serves 8–10.

For the *Clermont Bavarois* proceed as above, omitting the dried fruits, and using chopped *marrons glacés* instead. Flavour the custard with rum.

137

# Queen of Puddings

3 oz fresh, white breadcrumbs
3 eggs, separated
3½ oz sugar
¾ pint milk

1 oz butter
zest of a lemon
3 tablespoons raspberry jam

Simmer the lemon zest, devoid of white pith, in the milk for 5 minutes. Take out the zest, and add the butter and 1½ oz of the sugar, and cook until sugar and butter dissolve. Stir in the breadcrumbs and leave to cool. Beat the egg yolks, and add by degrees. Pour the mixture into a buttered 8-inch pie dish or Pyrex dish, and bake in an oven at 350° for 20 minutes, or until the custard has set. Beat the egg whites with rest of the sugar, whisking until peaks can be formed. Remove the pudding from the oven, and melt the jam in a small pan. Pour the jam over the surface of the custard, then arrange the meringue over all, roughening the surface into peaks with a fork. Return to the oven and bake until light brown. Serves 4-6.

# Réligieuse

choux pastry
shortcrust pastry (for pastry
   recipes, see pages 158–62)
6 oz sugar
1 heaped tablespoon of flour

8 eggs, separated
¾ pint milk
double cream
vanilla sugar or essence
chocolate and coffee icing

Line a 6-inch cake tin or flan tin with sweet shortcrust pastry, no higher than 1¼ inches; fill with beans, or line with foil, and bake blind. (Roughly 6 oz pastry will be required.) Make some éclairs to the recipe on page 163, pipe them so that they taper slightly towards one end, about 4½ inches long. Pipe a ring of paste 3½ inches across, another 2½ inches and a ball 1 inch. Make a St Honoré cream as follows: beat the sugar with the yolks of 6 eggs to a light cream; stir in the flour. Bring the milk to the boil and pour on the yolks and sugar. Return to the pan, and boil for 5 minutes. Add the vanilla flavouring and, when the custard is cool, fold in the stiffly whipped whites of the eggs, plus 2 extra whites. Fill the choux pastry shells with this cream, using a piping bag and plain nozzle. As for éclairs, coat each with chocolate icing and coffee icing alternately. Fill the shortcrust shell with the cream, building it into a cone, and assemble the éclairs, the thick ends resting on the edge of the pastry shell, tapering towards the top. Lay the wider choux ring on top, then the smaller, with the choux ball crowning the whole. The choux rings are decorated with chocolate and coffee icing. Serves 8–10.

## Tea Soufflé

This soufflé has the colour of *café au lait* while possessing the faint and delicate flavour of tea, in fact a French dish with a decided English influence.

| | |
|---|---|
| 1 *oz butter* | 2 *oz sugar* |
| 1 *oz flour* | 4 *egg yolks and* 5 *whites* |
| 3 *tablespoons milk* | *pinch of salt* |
| 1 *teacupful strong tea* | |

Make a roux with the butter and flour. Add the milk to make a stiffish paste, then add the tea by degrees, the aim being to achieve a thick sauce. Stir in the sugar and cook for 5 minutes. Allow the mixture to cool slightly, then add the beaten egg yolks. Whip the whites with the salt until firm but not too stiff. Prepare a soufflé dish, or individual dishes, buttering them and dusting them with sugar. Fold the egg whites into the sauce, but do not beat them in, and do not worry about a marbled effect. Pour into the soufflé dish and bake at 400° until well risen – about 20 minutes for individual soufflés, longer for large ones. A soufflé should be well risen, golden brown on top. It should be soft in the middle, even liquid, and this is a matter of taste and timing. Chefs usually dust the top with icing sugar, and glaze with a salamander or under a fierce grill before serving. This is only to be recommended with eye-level grills, or those with a large compartment. Serves 4–5.

## Summer Pudding

This pudding originated in the early 19th century in Malvern Spa, where it was served to those who came to take the waters. It was called, not surprisingly 'Malvern Pudding', but later became 'Hydropathic Pudding'. Only recently has it assumed its latest name of 'Summer Pudding'. It has been mistakenly supposed that the name 'Hydropathic Pudding' was due to the fact that bread is more easily digested than pastry, but variations of this ancient pudding are found far from spa resorts. Mrs Bridges calls it Malvern Pudding, and it was fairly local to her childhood home in Gloucestershire.

3 *lb fresh fruit (raspberries*     10 *oz caster sugar*
    *and redcurrants)*     *a dozen slices of white bread*

Use a 3-pint pudding basin and line it with the bread by cutting a disc of bread to fit the bottom, and placing wedge-shaped fingers of bread, each as long as the height of the basin, side by side to fit snugly; there should be no gaps. Wash the fruit and drain, stir in the sugar until it is dissolved, and taste for sweetness – ripe berries need quite a lot of sugar. Put the fruit in a pan, and simmer until tender, about 10 minutes, but add no water. Pour the fruit into the bowl and cover with a layer of bread to neatly fit the top. Put a plate on the top, one that fits into the basin, and put a weight on the plate to press down so that the pudding can cohere. Leave for several hours, and preferably overnight, in a cool place. To serve, run a thin-bladed knife around the pudding, and carefully invert on a serving dish. Serve with whipped cream. Serves 6–8.

# Syllabub

This recipe comes from Mrs Bridges' home town of Bristol, a place long noted for importing sherry, which plays an important part in good syllabubs.

4 *oz sugar*     1 *dessertspoon brandy*
½ *pint double cream*     *a large glass of sherry (about*
*juice of a lemon*     *4 tablespoons)*

Grate the rind of the lemon into the sugar and add the juice and sherry. Stir until the sugar is dissolved and pour in the brandy. Whip the cream until firm, and mix it into the rest and pour into tall glasses. The syllabubs should be left until the cream and wine separate, the cream rising to the top. Serve with macaroons. Serves 4–6.

# Tarte aux Framboises

For the pastry:
7 *oz flour*     1 *egg*
3 *oz butter*     1 *dessertspoon sugar*
*pinch of salt*     *iced water*

Rub the fat into the flour with the salt, and stir in the sugar. Beat the egg and add to the flour and mix. Add enough iced water to form a stiff dough, knead into a ball and leave to rest for an hour. Line a 9-inch tart or flan tin with the pastry, rolled out to ⅛-inch thick. Prick bottom of pastry with a fork, and bake blind (see recipe for Custard Tart, page 150).

Make a **Crème Pâtissière** as follows:

*2 oz sugar*  
*1 egg plus one yolk*

*1 oz flour plus ½ oz cornflour*  
*¾ pint milk*

Separate one egg, and blend the two yolks together with the sugar and the flour. Add a little milk to make a cream. Warm the rest of the milk and pour on the eggs and stir. Return to the pan and boil for 5 minutes. When cool, add the egg white whipped stiff. Spread the cream on the pastry shell and, before it has time to form a skin, cover with selected fresh or frozen raspberries, about 1½ lb. Glaze the raspberries with redcurrant jelly, slightly warmed. Leave to set for 1 hour. Serve with whipped cream. Serves 6–8.

# SAVOURIES

## The Upstairs Recipes

Angels on Horseback
Devils on Horseback
Kromeskies
Marrow Bones
Scotch Woodcock

## The Downstairs Recipes

Welsh Rarebit
Devilled Cheese

# Angels on Horseback

12 *oysters*  
6 *rashers streaky bacon*  
     *cayenne pepper*  
1 *lemon*

Cut and trim the rashers in halves, season with cayenne pepper, and wrap each oyster in bacon. They may be rolled and skewered, or tied with thread if necessary. Grill until browned, remove the thread or skewer and serve with lemon wedges. Serves 4.


# Devils on Horseback

12 *prunes*  
6 *rashers streaky bacon*  
12 *rolled anchovy fillets or*  
    *anchovy olives*  
    $\frac{1}{2}$ *pint water*  
    *toast or fried bread*

Soak the prunes for an hour in the water (or water plus a glass of red wine). Simmer in the water/wine until tender. Cool, remove the stones, and stuff with anchovies or olives. Trim the bacon and cut each rasher in half. Wrap around the prunes and grill as above. Serve prunes on squares of toast, or bread fried in butter. Serves 4.


# Kromeskies

A useful recipe for using up cooked meats – chicken, ham, turkey, etc.

8 *oz cooked meat*  
2 *oz mushrooms*  
4 *rashers streaky bacon*  
1 *oz butter*  
    *salt and pepper*  
    *thick Béchamel Sauce (see*  
      *page 26)*  
    *fritter batter*

Mince the meat, chop the mushrooms finely. Fry the mushrooms in butter, mix with the meat and season. Bind with a thick Béchamel, using the recipe on page 26, but with less milk. Shape into small croquettes on a floured surface. Cut each rasher in half, and wrap around the croquettes. Dip in fritter batter and fry in hot oil. Serves 4–6.

143

# Marrow Bones

beef marrow bones, cut into          hot, buttered toast
   2–3-inch lengths          salt, cayenne pepper

The ends of the bones need to be plugged to prevent the marrow escaping during cooking. One way is to wrap the ends in kitchen foil, and tie them securely. The old, established method is to plug the ends with thick flour paste. Steam them in a sieve or collander above boiling water for an hour. Serve them, the foil or paste removed, standing upright on a dish. Each person should have a marrow scoop, or thin bladed knife. The marrow is spread on the toast, and seasoned with salt and cayenne. Serve 2 or 3 bones per person.

# Scotch Woodcock

2 eggs                                   triangles of toast, spread with
1 oz butter                                 Patum Peperium or
¾ teacupful milk                            anchovy butter
salt and cayenne pepper

Make some triangles of thin toast, and spread with either Patum Peperium or anchovies pounded and mixed with butter. Beat the eggs with the milk, add seasoning. Melt the butter in a double boiler, pour in the eggs and milk, and stir until the mixture thickens – it may even curdle. Pour on to the toast and serve. Serves 4–6.

# Welsh Rarebit

8 oz cheese (preferably                  salt and pepper
   Cheddar)               small bottle dark beer
1 oz butter                              buttered toast
1 teaspoon mustard

Melt the cheese with the butter in a pan, add the mustard and the beer to make a thick, creamy sauce. Pour over the buttered toast, and quickly brown under the grill. Serves 4.

# Devilled Cheese

As above, but adding cayenne pepper, heaped teaspoon of dry mustard and 1 tablespoon of any hot pickle.

# PUDDINGS

## The Downstairs Recipes

Apple Charlotte
Apple Pie
Bread and Butter
  Pudding
Brown Bread
  Pudding with
  Whip Sauce
Custard Tart
Jam Roly-Poly
Jam Sponge
Shrove Tuesday
  Pancakes
Spotted Dick
Treacle Pudding
Treacle Tart
Trifle

# Apple Charlotte

4 *large Bramley apples*
5 *oz sugar*
1 *teaspoon vanilla sugar (or a few drops essence)*

*about* 18 *slices of white bread, cut* $\frac{1}{4}$*-inch thick*
4–5 *oz butter*

Peel and slice the apples, then cook them with sufficient water to make a thick purée with the sugar and the vanilla. The less water you can use, the better. Cut a small disc of greaseproof paper or foil to fit the bottom of a 2-pint basin or Charlotte mould, and butter it well. Melt the butter in a frying pan, cut the bread into fingers to fit the mould; they fit together without gaps if they are tapered like a wedge. Line the bottom and the sides with this buttered bread, and fill with the apple purée, covering with fingers of bread. Cover the mould with a lid or small baking sheet, and bake at 400° for 1 hour. Leave to cool for at least 30 minutes before turning out. Run a thin-bladed knife around the inside of the basin, and make sure that the bread is not sticking, then invert on to a serving dish with the greatest care. During the baking the sugar caramelises, and glues the bread to the basin, which can break the shape of the pudding. Serves 4–6.


# Apple Pie

8 *oz shortcrust pastry*
3 *lb mixed apples*
1 *lemon*

*cloves, cinnamon or nutmeg*
4–5 *oz sugar*

'An apple pie,' writes Mrs Bridges, 'should be full of fruit. It should not be too sweet, nor the fruit mushy. It should have a faint flavour of lemon or spice. If too much lemon is used, and the peel cut too thick, it may taste of turpentine. A mixture of cooking and eating apples can be used, for the eating apples hold their shape, while the cookers give that degree of tartness so essential to the true apple pie. A good Colville baking apple, for instance, with some Kentish Codlins or Ribston Pippins.' Today we would use a Bramley with some Cox's Pippins or Granny Smiths.

Peel and slice the apples, and cover them with a damp cloth. Put the cores and peelings with the lemon rind in a pan. Cover with water, and boil until a good juice has been obtained. Use a deep pie dish about 7 or 8 inches in diameter, and put the apples in it with a tablespoon of sugar to each layer. Add one or two cloves, or other spice according to taste. Strain the juice over the apples. Roll out the pastry, and cut a strip to fit the edge of the pie dish. Wet the edge, and press the pastry strip around. Moisten the pastry strip, lay the rolled-out pastry on top and press down, sealing with a fork, or crimping with the fingers. If the pie is really filled with apples, there is no need to use a pie funnel. Cut a few tiny slits in the pastry to permit steam to escape, dust with caster sugar, and put in an oven set at 400°. After about 20 minutes, when the pastry is golden brown, turn the heat down to 350° and cook for a further 15 minutes. Serves 4–6.

## Bread and Butter Pudding

There are several recipes for this pudding in Mrs Bridges' book. Bread and Butter Pudding as we know it today was sometimes called 'Wholesome Fare' pudding in the early 1900s, and 'bread and butter' pudding contained no fruit, but was often made with suet instead of butter.

*4 oz butter*
*5 eggs*
*1¾ pints creamy milk*
*3 oz each currants and*
  *sultanas*

*about 12 slices white bread*
*2 oz sugar*
*nutmeg (optional)*

Trim the crusts from the bread, butter a few slices thickly to cover the bottom of a baking dish or pie dish about 7 by 10 inches. Sprinkle some of the currants and sultanas over the bread. Butter some more slices, and lay these on top, sprinkling more fruit and so on, until the dish is full. The final layer should have no fruit on top, as it will burn during the baking. Make a custard with the milk, sugar and eggs, heating the milk to dissolve the sugar, and adding it to the eggs, well beaten. Pour over the bread until it has all been absorbed, and press the top layer down to fit snugly. Nutmeg can be grated on top if desired. Bake at 350° until well browned (about 1 hour). Serves 6–8.

## Brown Bread Pudding with Whip Sauce

*6 oz brown bread*
*¼ pint milk*
*grated rind of 1 lemon*

*4 eggs*
*2 oz soft brown sugar*

Tear the bread into small pieces. Boil the milk and pour it over the bread. Leave until the bread is soft and has absorbed the milk. Squeeze out excess moisture, and beat in the brown sugar with a fork. Add the grated lemon rind and the yolks of two eggs separated from the whites. Beat the other two eggs and add to the mixture, beating thoroughly. Put it into a 1½-pint Charlotte mould or basin, cover with greaseproof paper, then with a cloth tied around the top. Boil the pudding gently for 1¼ hours. Turn out and serve with Whip Sauce.

## Whip Sauce

Put the yolks of two eggs into a double boiler with a dessert-spoon of caster sugar and a glass of white wine (Sauternes or an English country wine, such as parsnip or cowslip),the grated rind of a lemon, and a small piece of cinnamon stick. Whisk over simmering water until the mixture thickens to a sauce. Serves 4–6.

## Custard Tart

8 *oz shortcrust pastry*       1½ *oz caster sugar*
3 *eggs*                        *grated nutmeg*
½ *pint milk*

Line a 6 or 7-inch flan or sandwich tin with the pastry, rolled out to ⅛ inch thick (take care not to stretch the pastry). Prick the bottom here and there with a fork, and cover with dried haricot beans, pieces of crust, or aluminium foil cut to fit. Bake blind at 400° for 10 minutes, remove beans or foil, and return to the oven for 3 or 4 minutes, or until the shell has coloured slightly. Heat the milk with the sugar, stirring until the sugar has dissolved. Remove from the heat, beat the eggs with a whisk until frothy, add to the milk. Pour the custard into the pastry case, grate nutmeg on top, place on the centre shelf of the oven, set at 300°, and bake until the custard has set – about 20 minutes. Serves 4–6.

# Jam Roly-Poly

A true, old-fashioned Roly-Poly must be boiled in a floured cloth, a practice avoided by cooks these days, who prefer to put the mixture in a pudding basin whence it loses its identity. 'When I was a girl, we used to boil our puddings on washday,' writes Mrs Bridges reflectively, 'because the smell of boiled puddings was like the smell of washing in the copper. If we were obliged to have one, we might as well have both.' It may be supposed that the pudding and the washing were not done in the same 'copper' vessel, but either way, it is hardly a recommendation for this otherwise excellent English pudding, a real 'rib-sticker'.

*1 lb suet crust pastry*       *raspberry or strawberry jam*

Roll out the suet crust to about $\frac{1}{4}$-inch thickness. 1 lb of pastry will serve six people, and you will require about $\frac{1}{2}$ lb of jam. Roll to an oblong shape, and spread with as much jam as you wish, to within $\frac{1}{2}$ inch of the edge all round. Roll up as for a Swiss Roll, seal the edges and close the ends. Take a clean cloth large enough to take the pudding, and wring it out in hot water. Spread it flat, and dust it liberally with flour. Roll the pudding in the cloth, tie both ends tightly with string. Lower it into a large pan of boiling water, with a trivet or inverted plate on the bottom. Let it boil continuously for $1\frac{1}{2}$ hours, adding extra boiling water from the kettle if needed. Serve with custard, or sweet white sauce, or jam sauce. Serves 6.

# Jam Sponge

*4 oz butter*       *$\frac{1}{2}$ teaspoon baking powder*
*2 oz caster sugar*       *pinch of salt*
*5 oz flour*       *three heaped tablespoons of*
*2 eggs*       *raspberry jam*
*$1\frac{1}{2}$ tablespoons milk*

Cream the butter and sugar and beat in the eggs, one at a time. Sift the flour with the baking powder and a pinch of salt, and fold into the batter. Grease a $2\frac{1}{2}$-pint pudding basin, and spread the jam on the bottom. Pour the batter over the jam. Cover with greaseproof paper or foil, thinly buttered, then with a damp cloth. Tie securely, taking the string over the top of the basin to serve as a handle. Place in a large pan containing sufficient boiling water to come threequarters of the way up the basin, reduce to low simmering, cover and steam for 1½ hours. Use a trivet on the bottom of the pan. Turn the pudding out on a serving dish and serve with custard sauce. Serves 4–6.

# Shrove Tuesday Pancakes

Shrove Tuesday was much more closely observed in Mrs Bridges' time, when preparations for Lent ensured that the eggs be used up for pancakes.

| | |
|---|---|
| 2 *eggs* | ¾ *pint milk* |
| 6 *oz flour* | 1 *oz melted butter* |
| *salt* | *nutmeg* |
| 1½ *oz caster sugar* | |

Put the flour, sieved with the salt, into a bowl. Break in the eggs and mix, adding the milk by degrees until a smooth batter is achieved. Pour in the melted butter and add the sugar; stir so that the batter is thoroughly mixed. Grate a little nutmeg in the batter, and place it in a cool place, covered, for at least an hour. When you come to make the pancakes, you may need to add more milk, as the flour will have absorbed the previous milk, and consequently the batter is thicker – it should resemble thin cream. The frying pan should be very hot, and lightly greased. Pour the batter in and swirl it round the pan, try and get it as thin as possible, don't worry about a lacey pattern full of holes, it is the lightness that counts. Fold each pancake, and serve with wedges of lemon and caster sugar. Makes 12 pancakes.

# Spotted Dick

Mrs Bridges' recipe, which is correct, calls for suet and flour with currants, a pale dough pudding spotted with black currants, which gives the pudding its name. Recently, the pudding has been accorded middle-class airs with raisins and sultanas set in a light sponge. Mrs Bridges wouldn't recognise it.

| | |
|---|---|
| 4 *oz flour* | 5 *oz currants* |
| 4 *oz suet* | 1 *teaspoon baking powder* |
| 4 *oz breadcrumbs* | *pinch of salt* |
| 2 *oz sugar* | |

Sieve the flour, salt and baking powder. Add the suet, finely grated, the breadcrumbs, sugar and currants. Mix to a stiff dough with water. Traditionally, and in Mrs Bridges' recipe, the dough is wrapped in a floured cloth, then tied in a ball and boiled. Otherwise put the dough in a buttered pudding basin and boil as in the recipe for Jam Sponge. Allow at least $2\frac{1}{2}$–3 hours' boiling in either case. Turn out and serve with Custard Sauce, or a sweetened white sauce flavoured with rum or brandy. Serves 6–8.

# Treacle Pudding

To Mrs Bridges, 'treacle' was golden syrup, and that which we call black treacle was known as 'molasses'. (Treacle Tart, for instance, is always made with golden syrup and not black treacle.)

| | |
|---|---|
| 6 *oz flour* | $\frac{1}{2}$ *teaspoon ginger* |
| 6 *oz fine breadcrumbs* | $\frac{1}{2}$ *teaspoon bicarbonate of soda* |
| 4 *oz suet* | 3 *tablespoons black treacle* |
| 1 *egg* | 1 *tablespoon milk* |

Sift the flour, mix with the breadcrumbs and finely grated suet and ginger. Add the egg, beaten; thin the treacle by warming it in a pan, and stir into the mixture. Dissolve the bicarbonate of soda in the milk and beat it in, adding extra milk if needed to make a stiffish dough. Put the dough in a well-buttered 2-pint pudding basin, cover with greaseproof paper or foil, then with a damp cloth. Tie under the rim securely with string, pass the string over the top of the pudding and tie for a handle – it makes it a simple matter to lift the pudding out. Steam in a covered pan for 3 hours. Serve with warmed treacle or golden syrup. Serves 6–8.

# Treacle Tart

| | |
|---|---|
| 8 *oz sweet shortcrust pastry* | $1\frac{1}{2}$ *oz fresh breadcrumbs* |
| *(see page* 159 *)* | *juice of* $\frac{1}{2}$ *lemon* |
| 6 *tablespoons golden syrup* | |

The traditional treacle tart is always made on a plate, never in a sandwich or flan tin, and decorated with a lattice of twisted pastry strips. Use a heatproof plate or enamelled tin plate about 8–9 inches diameter. Line the plate with the pastry, rolled out to

$\frac{1}{8}$-inch thickness, and scallop the edges. Combine the syrup, breadcrumbs and lemon juice, mix well and pour into the pastry. Cut some strips to fit across the plate in a lattice, twist and secure the ends by wetting with a pastry brush. Bake on centre shelf at 400° for 15 minutes. Reduce heat to 350°, and bake until pastry is golden. Serves 6–8.

# Trifle

The original trifle was a 'syllabub with sweetmeats added', and a close relation to the fruit fool. Gooseberry trifle, for instance, is simply stewed gooseberries blended with custard. Mrs Bridges' trifle contained sponge fingers, ratafias, macaroons, almonds, candied fruits, sherry, custard, cream, and sugar sweets and comfits to decorate the top. Here is one of her simpler recipes for the 'kitchen Sunday dinner'.

| | |
|---|---|
| 8 *sponge cakes* | 4 *oz blanched, halved almonds* |
| 1 *tablespoon caster sugar* | 10 *oz double cream* |
| 4 *tablespoons raspberry jam* | 1 *pint custard* |
| $\frac{3}{4}$ *lb fresh (or frozen)* | *sherry* |
| *raspberries* | |

Stale cake can be used instead of sponge cakes. Spread the cake, cut into slices an inch thick by two inches long, or the sponge cakes split in halves, with raspberry jam. Sandwich the jam surfaces together, and cut the slices into cubes or fingers. Lay some at the bottom of a glass dish, and douse them liberally with sherry; scatter some of the raspberries and some of the almonds on the sponges. Now have another layer of sponge, and more raspberries and almonds until the bowl is threequarters filled, sprinkling the layers with sherry. Reserve some almonds for decoration. Have the custard ready, and pour it over the sponges, moving them aside here and there with a knife, so that the custard penetrates throughout. Allow the custard to set. Take the double cream, and whip until stiff, fold in a heaped tablespoon of caster sugar, and spread the cream over the custard. Decorate the surface with almonds and, if liked, strips of angelica and halved glacé cherries. Serves 6–8.

# BREAD, CAKES AND PASTRY

'The British,' quoth Mrs Bridges, 'and in particular Scotch women, are the finest bakers in the world!' She would have got an argument from the Germans, the Austrians and the French, who would have produced Sacher-Torte and Mille Feuilles in answer to Victoria Sponge and Shortbread. Nevertheless, a delicious and yeasty aroma must have pervaded Eaton Place on baking days. From the kitchen came home-baked breads, Vienna twists, meringues, brioches and éclairs – Mrs B knew more than a thing or two about Continental pastries. In response to the British demand for British things, and the appetites of all at Eaton Place, Mrs Bridges made Battenberg Cake, Walnut and Windsor Cakes, Dundee and Dripping, Madeira and Marble. From the bread oven came Chelsea Buns and Bath Buns, cottage loaves and soda bread, tea rings and Lardy Cake.

Judging by the number of recipes given, it would seem that bread dough rose through the roof of Eaton Place, but the main reason was due to the recent vogue for 'afternoon tea'. 'These

155

recipes are given in the hope that they may prove of great service and benefit to households both in town and country, where afternoon tea is a daily institution of considerable importance . . . now that the fashionable dinner hour has come to be so late.' Ladies of leisure and quality assuaged their delicate appetites with dainty sandwiches and slices of cherry cake. The tea-time habit created a demand for different cakes and new recipes, which were available in a variety unknown a mere thirty years before; few cakes were featured in Mrs Beeton's original book, but by the time Mrs Bridges published hers she was able to include the latest fancies from across the Atlantic – New York Cakes, Boston Tea Cake and Boston Brownies, Angel's Food Cake and Florida Cake, Kentucky Cake and Wisconsin Bread. Mrs Bridges probably cut the recipes out of *Home Notes* or *The Queen* to which the Bellamys would have certainly subscribed.

There are interesting cakes from various counties in England with which she had been associated. With the recipe for Bedfordshire Wigs, Tander and Cattern Cakes, she writes 'My mother was a Bedford woman, and she taught me these recipes. In those days they had harvest cakes called 'Fourses', because they were round cakes divided up into four pieces, although some folk say it is because they are eaten at four of the clock. The farmers' wives baked Wigs, that were supposed to curl up over the edge of the tin like an old-fashion gentleman's powdered wig, but I never made one that curled in this fashion. Anyway, we used to eat them with hot elder wine.' From Southwold comes the recipe for Wiltshire Lardy Cake, and Sally Lunns from nearby Bath – and, of course, the famous bun.

We do not know if Mrs B was a good pastrycook. She gives recipes for Mille Feuilles which require light, flaky pastry. She made éclairs, with choux paste, cream horns, pudding and pies, with puff and shortcrust. But the proof is in the eating, and some cooks possess the light-fingered touch while others do not; pastry-cooks are a breed apart. One can, of course, buy pastry ready made, but it is usually not quite as rich as home-made pastry, and one is cheated of the satisfaction of watching one's own creative efforts coming crisp, light and golden from the oven. Mrs Bridges was down in the kitchen at six in the morning, 'to make the pastry while the kitchen is still cool. To make good pastry you need cool, light hands, and cool ingredients. Sift your flour several times, and squeeze all moisture from butter and lard [this was 1900, remember]. Lemon juice will make your pastry light, and if the household possesses a refrigerator, return the paste to cool before using.'

# BREAD, CAKES & PASTRY

## Basic Recipes for Pastry and Dough

Hot Water Pastry
Shortcrust Pastry
Puff Pastry

Rich Puff Pastry
 or Pâte Feuilletée
Choux Pastry

## The Upstairs Recipes

*Pastry*
Éclairs
Mille Feuilles

*Bread and Buns*
Making Bread
Bath Buns
Brioche

Sally Lunns
Plaited Tea Bread

*Cakes*
Making Cakes
Angel Cake
Battenberg Cake
Boston Brownies
Cherry Cake
Chocolate Cake
Christmas Cake
Dundee Cake

Madeira Cake
My Lady's Cake
Meringues
New York Cake
Victoria Sponge
Glacé Icing
Royal Icing

# Hot Water Pastry for Raised Pies

The pie-making area of England stretches across the Midlands into the Welsh border, where they make the finest pork pies in the world. Mrs Bridges' pies were obviously in great demand. She uses a 'stone of flour, a good handful of salt, ten pounds of fine pork'. The proportions for hot water pastry are usually one third of fat to the quantity of flour, and water to make a workable paste.

12 *oz flour*          5 *oz water*
4 *oz lard*           1 *level teaspoon salt*

Boil water and lard together until the lard melts completely. Sieve the flour with the salt into a bowl, make a well in the centre of the flour, pour in the hot liquid and mix with a wooden spoon. Knead lightly until smooth and leave in a warm place for thirty minutes. To shape the dough, reserve a piece for the pie lid, make the rest into a ball, flatten slightly with your hand. In place of a traditional wooden pie mould use a milk bottle, half-filled with warm water. Press the base into the dough, bringing the paste up the bottle to about $3\frac{1}{2}$ inches high, turning it as you raise the paste. The pastry should be $\frac{1}{4}$-inch thick, or slightly less – enough to support the filling. An alternative method is to line a small, straight-sided baking tin. When your pie is filled, cover with the lid and seal and crimp the edges. Game pies were often made with this pastry, in a fluted mould, and decorated with pastry leaves.

# Shortcrust Pastry

8 *oz plain flour*  
4 *oz butter or lard*

*pinch of salt*  
*about 4 tablespoons iced water*

Sieve the flour with the salt, cut the butter into small pieces and rub it into the flour to a consistency of fine breadcrumbs, using the tips of the fingers. Make a well in the mixture, and add the water. Mix together, and turn out on to a floured slab or board, and knead lightly until the dough is well cohered and smooth. Allow the pastry to rest in a cool place for at least 30 minutes before using; this prevents the paste from shrinking during cooking and the edge of the pie falling into the contents to ruin it, a familiar experience with many cooks. For a rich pastry, and one for tarts and fruit pies, add an extra 2 oz of butter, and a heaped teaspoon or two of caster sugar, plus the yolk of an egg, but use slightly less water.

# Puff Pastry

8 *oz plain flour*  
6 *oz butter*

*pinch of salt*  
4–5 *tablespoons iced water*

Sift flour and salt together, cut the butter into small pieces and rub it into the flour to a consistency of fine breadcrumbs. Make a well in the mixture, and pour in 3 tablespoons of iced water, and work the mixture into a ball. If the mixture is too crumbly, add more iced water until it all coheres. Leave to rest for 30 minutes. Roll the dough on a floured slab or board, into a rectangle about 1-inch thick. Dust with flour, roll into an oblong twice the length of the width. Fold one third over, then the remaining third over that. With one of the open ends towards you, roll away from you into another oblong – say, 7 inches wide by 20 inches long. Repeat the folding process, dusting with flour, and roll again, keeping the open end towards you. Do not turn the pastry over, and always try to roll it in the same direction. Do not let the rolling pin stray over the far or near edge of the pastry, other-

wise it will begin to lose its rectangular shape. Ideally, the pastry should rest for 10 minutes between each fold and turn – three in all. A richer pastry can be made by using more fat, equal proportions of fat to flour.

# Rich Puff Pastry, or Pâte Feuilletée

8 oz plain flour
½ teaspoon of salt
8 oz butter, softened to a
   workable consistency

1 teaspoon of fresh lemon juice
about ¼ pint or less of iced
   water

Sift the flour and salt into a mixing bowl. Add the lemon juice and the water and 2 oz butter. Mix well together and knead into a dough. If it crumbles, add more iced water by degrees, taking care not to over-moisten the dough. Put the dough on to a floured board, and roll into a square, about ½-inch thick. Leave it to rest for 30 minutes. Place the rest of the butter on a piece of grease-proof paper, and shape into a square. Place another piece of paper on top, and roll into a square the size of the pastry. The butter and pastry should be of the same consistency, neither too soft nor too hard. Roll the dough into a larger square, about 12–14 inches. Place the square of butter in the centre, and fold the sides of the dough to meet in the centre. Now fold the ends of the dough to meet each other in the centre. The butter is now enclosed in the pastry, parcel-wrapped. Flour very sparingly the parcel of dough – or 'book', as Mrs Bridges called it, keeping the open end towards you. Now roll away from you, into an oblong. Fold one end in towards the middle, and the other end over that, so you have a three-layer rectangle. Leave to rest for 10–15 minutes. Repeat the rolling and folding process, with rests in between, for 6 rollings in all. If the butter breaks through the surface, dust the fracture with flour, and return to the refrigerator for 20 minutes, before rolling again.

# Choux Pastry

4 oz plain flour
3 oz butter

½ pint water
4 eggs

Put the water and the butter into a pan and bring to the boil. When the butter has melted, remove from the heat and add the flour, all at once, and beat into a stiff dough with a wooden spoon, until the paste leaves the sides of the pan. Beat the eggs thoroughly, and add to the dough a little at a time. It may not be necessary to add all the egg, but sufficient to give the dough a piping consistency.

# Éclairs

Take a quantity of choux paste, and pipe it through a forcing bag to 4-inch lengths, on a greased baking sheet. Keep the shapes even, using a wet knife to cut the paste from the piping nozzle, and to shape the paste should it go awry. Bake at 400° until the éclairs are well risen and golden – about 30 minutes. Put them on a wire cake rack, and make a slit in the side of each to permit the steam to escape. When they are cold, fill with whipped cream or *crème pâtissière*. Cover the top of each éclair with chocolate or coffee icing.

# Mille Feuilles

Mrs Bridges' original recipe for *mille feuilles* is rather different from those rectangles of puff pastry, filled with whipped cream and jam, and decorated with *glacé* icing, with which we are familiar. Her *mille feuilles* is a single cake, with layers of puff pastry filled with apricot jam, and covered with meringue. Here is the modern recipe.

| | |
|---|---|
| *6 oz puff pastry* | *glacé icing* |
| *whipped cream or crème* | |
| *  pâtissière* | |

Roll out the dough to $\frac{1}{8}$-inch thickness into a large rectangle. Set the oven at 425°. Put the pastry on a prepared baking sheet, prick all over with a fork. Chill for 5 minutes. Bake in the oven until well risen and lightly browned, for 12–15 minutes. Turn the pastry over and bake a further 5 minutes.

Put the pastry on a cake rack to cool, and then cut in strips 2 inches wide. Trim any irregular edges, and spread one layer with pastry cream or whipped cream. Place another layer on top, also spread with cream. Top with a final layer, press gently and trim if necessary. Coat tops with *glacé* icing. In Paris, *mille feuilles* are often just sprinkled with icing sugar. In England, they are sandwiched with jam and whipped cream, and iced.

# Making Bread

While pastry should be kept as cool as possible while it is being made, bread needs warmth. Have the mixing bowl warm, the flour, water and the kitchen, too. Bread recipes need 'strong' flour, bread flour with a high content of gluten. In Mrs Bridges' day nearly all flour was bread flour, sometimes gritty with being stone-ground, and a lot of sieving was required. Today's household flours are perfect for cakes and puddings, but if you want a strong flour you have to ask for it. Yeast is widely obtainable in tins, but fresh baker's yeast is not so easy, unless you know of a baker who bakes on the premises. Most bread recipes, however, are for fresh yeast, since dried yeast quantities vary with the manufacturer. To get the yeast working, mix it with a little warmed milk or water and a teaspoon of sugar, and pour this into a well in the flour. Leave for 15 minutes, or until the yeast

is dissolved and frothy. Add the rest of the liquid, and mix to a dough. Knead the dough to ensure that the yeast is evenly distributed, knead with the heel of the hand, using both hands and working the dough away from you. After kneading, let the dough rise under a warm cloth in the bowl. The bowl should be well buttered, the surface of the dough well floured. The longer the dough takes to rise, the better the bread, it can be left overnight, or for as little as half an hour. Knead the dough lightly, known as 'knocking back', and shape as required. At this stage it can be put into warmed baking tins if you are making tin loaves. Let it 'prove', a second rise of 10 minutes or so, and bake in a hot oven, 450° for 10 minutes, and then 400° for the rest of the baking period. Test to see if the loaves are ready by tapping them underneath – if they sound hollow, the bread is done.

## Bath Buns

10 oz flour
salt
¼ pint milk
½ oz yeast
2 oz butter

2 oz caster sugar
1 egg
2 oz sultanas
1 oz candied peel
cube sugar

Sift the flour with a half teaspoon of salt. Cream the yeast with a little warmed milk and a teaspoon of sugar. Pour into the flour and leave to work. Heat the rest of the milk with the butter and sugar until the butter has melted and add to the yeast; it must not become too hot, but bearable to a finger dipped in it. Beat the egg and add to the mixture, and beat all together with a wooden spoon. The mixture will be a very soft and sticky dough. Leave to rise for 2 hours, knock back, and work in the sultanas and the peel. Leave to rise again for 30 minutes. Knock back once more, and flour a working surface. Drop quantities of the dough on to the board. As they are sticky, roll lightly in flour, and toss between the hands. Keep the balls of dough measuring roughly 2 inches, this will give a sizeable bun when baked. Try to prevent the sultanas or peel breaking through the surface while shaping. Put the dough on a prepared baking sheet, brush with egg and milk glaze, and place a few pieces of crushed lump sugar and candied peel on top of each. Bake in an oven set at 375° for 20 minutes. Before they are cool, brush buns with sugar syrup. This is not traditional with Bath Buns, but it improves appearance.

# Brioche

8 oz plain flour
7 oz butter
¼ oz yeast

½ teaspoon salt
2 teaspoons caster sugar
3 eggs

Sift the flour and the salt into a bowl. Cream the yeast with a little warmed milk and a half teaspoon of the sugar. Pour into a well in the flour and leave to work. Add the eggs, well beaten, the sugar, and mix to a dough with a wooden spoon. Now add the butter, softened, by degrees, beating it well into the dough. Using a fork, lift the dough, which will be very soft and sticky, high above the bowl, beating air into it. Cover and leave to rise for 2 hours. Knock back, cover again, and leave during the day or overnight; brioches should be prepared well in advance, for they repay long rising. Shape the dough as required, leave to prove for 30 minutes, and bake in a hot oven, 450°, until well risen, and golden brown.

# Sally Lunns

Sally Lunns were originally dough cakes, split while hot into two halves, and spread with butter. In Mrs Bridges' recipe, they are divided into three, toasted, spread with butter and reassembled. Traditionally, they are not iced.

¾ lb flour
2 oz butter
¾ oz yeast
pinch of salt

1 egg
¼ pint milk
1 tablespoon sugar

Sieve the flour with the salt and put in a low oven for a few minutes to warm. Cream the yeast with a teaspoon of sugar and a little warmed milk. When it has dissolved, take the flour from the oven, pour the yeast in the centre, and leave to work until frothy – about 15 minutes. Put the butter in the rest of the milk, add the sugar and heat until both dissolve. Let the mixture cool until tepid, add the egg well beaten, and pour into the flour. Mix to a dough using more milk if needed, the dough should be fairly soft and sticky. Beat or knead on a floured board until smooth, and leave in a warm place to rise for about an hour. Knock back, and divide the dough into two equal pieces. Put each into separate Sally Lunn or Charlotte tins of 5-inch diameter, and leave them for 15 minutes to prove. Glaze with egg and milk, or milk. Bake at 425° for 25 minutes, or until risen and brown on top.

## Plaited Tea Bread

1 *lb flour*
1 *oz yeast*
*level teaspoonful salt*
2 *eggs*

2 *oz butter*
$\frac{1}{4}$ *pint milk*
*sugar*

Sift the flour with the salt. Place in a large bowl and warm in oven. Cream the yeast with a little warm milk and teaspoonful of sugar. Make a well in the flour, pour in yeast and leave to work. After 20 minutes, when the yeast is spongy and frothy, add the beaten eggs and some of the milk, warmed to tepid. Mix to a dough, work in the butter, previously softened, add more milk if required. Make a soft dough, and knead until smooth. Clean the mixing bowl, butter it well, put the dough in and brush the surface of the dough with melted butter. Cover with a warm cloth, and leave to rise. After about 3 hours, knock back, and leave overnight. Set the oven to 425°. Knock back the dough again, knead lightly, and divide into two halves. Take each half and divide it into three. Roll out the pieces into even lengths, pulling and rolling until you have three rolls of dough each about 12 inches long. Taper the ends of each roll. Press one end of each piece together, and plait the three pieces. Secure the ends carefully, so that the loaf won't come unplaited in the baking. Leave to prove in a warm place for 20 minutes, brush with egg and milk, or milk glaze, and bake until well risen and brown – about 25 minutes. Glaze the unbrowned parts during the last 5 minutes of baking.

# Making Cakes

Most modern cake recipes call for self-raising flour, which contains bicarbonate of soda and cream of tartar as a raising agent, but in Mrs Bridges' time it was something of a novelty, and cake recipes asked that cooks add their own baking powder – which amounted to more or less the same thing. By itself, bicarbonate of soda has no value as a raising agent, it needs to be mixed with an acid, such as vinegar, cream of tartar, black treacle – all liberate carbon dioxide which makes the cake rise. You can also use *sal volatile* (ammonium carbonate) to achieve the same result, causing the house to smell of ammonia, even though it does not affect the taste of the cake. Other means of leavening are by beating air into the cake mixture, or by folding in stiffly beaten egg whites, or by yeast. Do not confuse bicarbonate of soda with baking powder. The amounts given in recipes are usually precise, and too much bicarbonate will give the cake a lingering, salty taste; half a teaspoonful is usually quite sufficient.

It is important to beat the butter and sugar together to the consistency of whipped cream – light and fluffy. Recipes always demand caster sugar, unless other kinds are clearly specified. Softened butter is easier to cream, so make sure it has not just come straight from the fridge, and likewise the eggs which, if too cold, may make the butter cream curdle. Use unsalted butter, as certain types are particularly salty, especially Welsh and Irish butters. Add the eggs, well beaten, to the butter by degrees. Always sift the flour, as it helps to introduce air into the mixture, and always fold it into the batter, don't beat it in. The batter should be of a soft dropping consistency, unless the recipe says otherwise. 'Soft dropping consistency' means that it falls fairly easily from the spoon, but is still thick enough to hold its shape. Tossing the dried fruit in flour prevents the fruit from sinking to the bottom of the cake during baking. Deep cake tins should be lined with buttered greaseproof paper, or buttered and sprinkled with flour. Bake cakes in the centre of the oven on the centre shelf. To test if they are cooked, insert a fine skewer into the centre of the cake. If the skewer comes away clean, with no batter or crumbs clinging to it, then the cake is done. Leave the cake in the tin to cool, before turning out on a wire cake rack.

The following recipes use plain flour, unless otherwise specified.

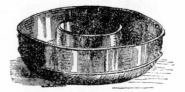

# Angel Cake

Mrs Bridges refers to this recipe as 'Angel's Cake from America'. Traditionally, this cake is not cut, but pulled apart with forks. Not, however, Mrs Bridges' cake: '. . . any cake that comes from *my* kitchen will not be torn up by forks,' she says firmly. The success of this cake, which requires not a few egg whites, depends on the ingredients being well sifted. Mrs Bridges' recipe uses 10 eggs, but the quantities given below are halved, making one substantial cake.

| | |
|---|---|
| 5 *egg whites* | *flavouring essence, vanilla or* |
| 5 *oz caster sugar* | *almond* |
| 1½ *oz each of cornflour and* | salt |
| *fine, plain flour* | *level teaspoon cream of tartar* |

Sift the flour 3 or 4 times. Beat the egg whites with a pinch of salt and cream of tartar until peaks are formed, but do not beat them too dry. Sift the sugar 3 times. Gently, and by degrees, fold in the sugar, adding the essence as required. Sift the flour over the mixture, folding it in by degrees, until all is incorporated. Pour the mixture into an ungreased savarin mould, or angel cake tin, and bake at 350° for 30 minutes, or until the surface of the cake springs back when pressed with a finger. Leave in the tin until cold, then turn out and decorate with flavoured *glacé* icing.

# Battenberg Cake

| | |
|---|---|
| 3 *eggs and their weight in* | *a little milk* |
| *butter, sugar and self-* | *pink food colouring* |
| *raising flour* | *apricot jam* |
| salt | 1½ *lb marzipan* |

Cream the butter and sugar until light and fluffy. Beat the eggs thoroughly, and add them by degrees to the butter mixture. Sift the flour and the salt and gently stir into the mixture, adding milk if required, to make a dropping consistency. From this batter, two separate cakes are to be baked. Use an oblong baking tin about 9 by 5 or 10 by 6 inches. Use a rectangle of baking foil to cover the bottom of the tin, large enough to be folded down the centre to make a division the same depth as that of the tin. You now have, in effect, two narrow baking tins. Pour half of the batter into one division. Colour the other half pink with the food colouring. Pour into the remaining division. Bake at 350° until the cake is done—test with a skewer. When the cakes are cool, remove them, and cut each down the centre, along its length. You now have four long pieces of cake, two yellow and two pink. Lay a yellow strip next to a pink one, and join together with apricot jam.

Place a pink length of cake on a yellow, and fit the remaining piece next to it, brushing all surfaces to be joined with apricot jam, the result being a chequered cake. Next, coat the cake in marzipan, made as follows:

| | |
|---|---|
| 12 *oz ground almonds* | 1 *teaspoon orange flower* |
| 6 *oz caster sugar* | *water* |
| 6 *oz icing sugar* | *juice of one small lemon* |
| 1 *egg* | *almond essence* |

Mix the dry ingredients together, then add the beaten egg, the orange flower water, essence and lemon juice to work to a smooth paste.

Roll out the paste to a rectangle of sufficient dimensions to wrap round the cake, brush the sponge with jam, enclose the cake with marzipan, leaving the ends open. Score a lattice pattern on the paste with a sharp knife and crimp the edges of the cake.

## Boston Brownies

| | |
|---|---|
| 4 *oz flour* | 2 *oz plain chocolate* |
| 4 *oz butter* | $\frac{1}{2}$ *teaspoon baking powder* |
| 8 *oz sugar* | $\frac{1}{2}$ *teaspoon salt* |
| 2 *eggs* | *vanilla essence or sugar* |
| 4 *oz chopped walnuts* | |

Melt chocolate in a pan with a dessertspoon of water, stirring constantly, but do not allow to boil. Cream the butter and sugar, beat the eggs and add them by degrees to the butter mixture, then add the chocolate. Sift flour, baking powder and salt together, and blend well with the chocolate mixture. Stir in the essence and the nuts. Pour into a greased, square cake tin and bake at 350° for about 30 minutes. When cold, cut into squares.

# Cherry Cake

12 *oz flour*  
8 *oz butter*  
8 *oz sugar*  
8 *oz glacé cherries*

*grated rind of ½ lemon*  
3 *large eggs*  
1 *teaspoon baking powder*  
2 *tablespoons milk*

Cream the butter and sugar, beat the eggs and add them a little at a time. Sift the flour with the baking powder, fold into the mixture. Grate the rind into the mixture, and beat to a dropping consistency, adding the milk if needed, but do not make it too soft. Cut the *glacé* cherries in half, and roll them in flour, adding them to the mixture. Pour into a prepared 8-inch cake tin and put on a centre shelf in the oven, set at 350° and bake for 1½ hours. Test with a skewer to see if cake is done. Leave to cool in the tin before turning out.

# Chocolate Cake

'One of the most enduringly popular of all cakes, and recipes are very varied,' comments Mrs Bridges, in the original Introduction to the Cake Chapter, 'and often spoiled through ignorance, even wilfulness. Chocolate cake must *never* be flavoured with anything other than vanilla. Some cooks ruin good chocolate cake by adding grated orange peel, or rum, or even coffee.'

3 *oz flour*  
6 *oz butter*  
3 *oz sugar*  
3 *oz ground almonds*  
4 *oz plain dessert chocolate*

4 *eggs*  
*vanilla essence or sugar*  
½ *teaspoon baking powder*  
1 *heaped tablespoonful cocoa*

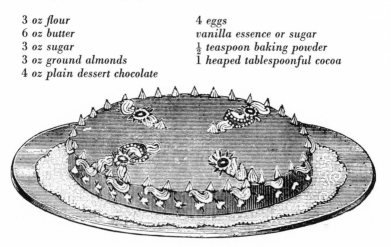

Melt the chocolate in a pan with a little water, stirring until smooth. Cream the butter and sugar. Separate the yolks of the eggs from the whites, add the yolks one by one to the butter cream. Add chocolate and a touch of vanilla. Sift the flour with the baking powder and cocoa, and add to the batter with the ground almonds. Beat all thoroughly, then whip the egg whites until stiff, and gently fold into the mixture. Pour into a prepared 7-inch cake tin, and bake for 1 hour at 300°, or until a skewer comes away clean. Coat with chocolate *glacé* icing.

## Christmas Cake

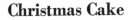

8 *oz flour*
7 *oz soft brown sugar*
10 *oz butter*
10 *oz finely grated candied*
   *peel*
10 *oz sultanas*
8 *oz currants*
5 *oz raisins*

4 *oz glacé cherries*
4 *oz chopped angelica*
4 *eggs*
*glass of brandy*
$\frac{1}{2}$ *teaspoon baking powder*
*salt*
5 *oz ground almonds*

Cream the butter and sugar, add the ground almonds, then the eggs, well beaten. Put all the fruit and peel into a bowl and toss them in flour until well coated, using about 2 oz of the flour. Sift the rest of the flour with baking powder and salt and fold into the creamed butter mixture. Now stir in the fruit, add the brandy and pour into an 8-inch cake tin lined with a band of greaseproof paper, buttered and floured. See that the paper stands 2 inches above the rim of the tin. Bake on a middle shelf at 310° for $1\frac{3}{4}$ hours, then lower to 290° and continue baking for $2\frac{1}{2}$ hours, testing with a skewer. Leave the cake to cool in the tin before turning out.

Refer to the recipe for Battenberg Cake, and brush the top of the Christmas Cake with apricot glaze, then with the marzipan recipe given for the Battenberg. Lay the marzipan on top of the cake and roll across with a rolling pin to about $\frac{1}{2}$-inch thick. Press the overlapping marzipan down and around the sides of the cake, using the rolling pin to give a clean, sharp finish. Allow the cake to rest for at least 48 hours before icing.

# Dundee Cake

10 oz flour
8 oz butter
7 oz sugar
4 oz ground almonds
4 oz each currants, raisins
   and candied peel

5 eggs
10 glacé cherries
grated rind of an orange
½ teaspoon baking soda
½ teaspoon salt
2 oz split, blanched almonds

Cream the butter and sugar. Beat the eggs and sift the flour, and add alternately to the butter cream, beating thoroughly. Stir in the washed and floured fruit and the *glacé* cherries, cut in halves. Add the ground almonds, salt and grated rind. Mix the bicarbonate of soda with a little milk, and stir into the mixture, beating in well. Pour into a prepared 8-inch cake tin. Lay the split almonds in a decorative circular pattern on the batter, and put the tin in an oven set at 300°. Bake on the middle shelf for 1½ hours, test with a skewer. Leave the cake to cool for 15 minutes in the tin, then turn out on to a cake rack.

# Madeira Cake

'Regularly served at Southwold in the mornings, was a slice or two of this cake with a glass of Madeira wine, which is how the cake got its name.' It is certainly true that the cake was so called because of the Victorian habit of serving a glass of Madeira wine as an accompaniment, but whether or not the habit started at Southwold with Mrs Bridges' cake must be left for historians to decide.

8 oz flour
8 oz butter
5 eggs
8 oz sugar

grated rind of a lemon
2 level teaspoons baking
   powder
candied lemon peel

Cream the butter and sugar in a bowl, beat the eggs and add them gradually to the creamed butter. Add the lemon rind, sift the flour and baking powder, and beat into the mixture by degrees. Pour into an 8-inch prepared cake tin. Bake at 350° for 30 minutes, and place two slices of candied peel in the centre of the cake. Bake a further 30 minutes, test with a skewer, and leave to cool before removing from the tin.

# My Lady's Cake

'This was Lady Wanborough's favourite cake,' writes Mrs Bridges, 'it was always requested when she came to tea.'

4 oz flour (self-raising)
2 oz butter
4 oz sugar

3 egg whites
1 tablespoon single cream
vanilla essence

Cream the butter and sugar, add the cream, and the vanilla flavouring. Beat the egg whites until stiff, sift the flour. Fold in the flour and egg whites alternately; whisk lightly. Put into a prepared 7-inch tin and bake at 350° for 40 minutes. The result will be an extremely light, open textured sponge. Split in two and spread with coffee butter cream, replace the two halves, and ice with coffee *glacé* icing, decorate with walnuts.

# Meringues

whites of 4 eggs                8 oz caster sugar

The best way to whisk egg whites is with a balloon whisk or failing that, a fork. Mrs Bridges always used a copper bowl and a whisk, although rotary whisks had been invented. The trouble with rotary whisks and electric mixers is they tend to over-whisk the whites, with the result that they become dry. Whites should be whisked up to the point where they hold their shape, and will not fall when held over the bowl. Having achieved this, fold in the sugar by degrees, making sure the mixture is smooth and even. Meringue may be piped in shapes, or moulded with a spoon. Butter a piece of greaseproof paper and dredge with flour. Lay the meringues on the paper placed on a baking sheet.

Put them in a very slow oven at 250°, and bake until they are a pale fawn colour. Ideally, they should be crisp on the outside, and toffee-like within. The pure white meringues purchased in commercial bakeries are usually made with icing sugar, and are baked so hard that they become powdery. Meringues are inclined not to keep for long, so eat them the day they are made. To serve for tea, join each meringue together with whipped, sweetened cream, flavoured with vanilla.

# New York Cake

This recipe was brought to Eaton Place by an American friend of the Bellamys, the heiress Harriet van Loon of White Plains, New York. Mrs Bridges writes, 'Mrs Van Loon's recipe, a cake with whiskey'. Mrs Bridges' recipe contains brandy, while the original probably required bourbon whiskey, an ingredient doubtless absent from the cellars of Eaton Place. This recipe reverts to the original.

8 oz flour
5 oz butter
5 oz sugar
vanilla essence
3 eggs

1 tablespoon bourbon whiskey
2 oz glacé cherries
2 oz flaked almonds
2 teaspoons baking powder

Cream the butter and sugar until light and fluffy. Separate the eggs. Lightly beat the yolks and add gradually to the butter cream. Add the whiskey, sift the flour and baking powder. Beat the egg whites until stiff. Toss the halved cherries in a little flour. Add the flour and the egg whites alternately, folding into the mixture. Now mix the cherries and the flaked almonds; flavour with a few drops of vanilla essence. Pour the mixture into an 8-inch square cake tin, and bake at 350° for 45 minutes, or until well risen and golden. Leave to cool in the tin, turn out on a wire cake rack and, when cold, cover with white *glacé* icing.

# Victoria Sponge Sandwich

The classic recipe for a Victoria Sponge is that the weight of the separate ingredients equals the combined weight of the eggs. Thus, the weight of 3 medium-size eggs, or 'standard' eggs would be about 6 oz, and so you would require 6 oz each of flour, sugar and butter. Cream the butter and the sugar, beat the eggs and add them slowly by degrees. Sift the flour (use self-raising; or plain flour with 2 teaspoons baking powder) with the salt, and beat into the mixture. Add enough milk to make a soft dropping consistency, and pour into prepared 7-inch sandwich tins. Bake at 350° for 30–40 minutes, or until a skewer comes out clean. When cold, sandwich together with raspberry jam, and whipped sweet cream, dust the top with sifted icing sugar.

# Glacé Icing

To every 8 oz of icing sugar, add 3–4 tablespoons of water, so that the icing is thick enough to coat the back of the spoon. Put the sugar and water into a small pan and warm gently, but do not allow it to get hot, otherwise the icing will become dull. Coffee Glacé Icing is made by adding enough strong, black coffee to flavour, in which case very little or no water at all is used. Chocolate Glacé Icing requires about 3 oz of melted bitter chocolate, or two heaped teaspoons of cocoa. A 7–8-inch cake needs about 4 oz of icing sugar.

# Royal Icing

'People have been known to break their teeth on wedding cakes,' warns Mrs Bridges, mindful of the fact that some icings are rock hard. Royal icing should be made in the proportions of 2 egg whites to each 1 lb of icing sugar. Separate the whites from the yolks, and beat the whites with a fork until frothy but not stiff. Fold in the sifted sugar, and add a dessertspoon of lemon juice. A tablespoon of glycerine ensures that the icing won't break any teeth, so beat it in with the sugar. Leave the icing in a covered bowl for 20 minutes before icing the cake. Leave the iced cake overnight before decorating.

# BREAD, CAKES & PASTRY

## The Downstairs Recipes

*Pastry*
Eccles Cakes
Jam Tarts
Mince Pies

*Bread and Buns*
Chelsea Buns
Cottage Loaf
Bedfordshire Wigs
Soda Bread
Lardy Cake

*Cakes*
Dripping Spice Cake
Gingerbread
Cornflour Cake
Rock Cakes
Scones
Seed Cake
Vinegar Cake

# Eccles Cakes

8 *oz flaky pastry*
4 *oz currants*
1 *oz butter*
1 *oz candied peel*

1 *oz soft brown sugar*
*grated nutmeg*
*egg white*

Melt butter and add the fruit, peel (finely chopped), the sugar and a little grated nutmeg. Add a little water if the filling is not moist enough. Roll out the pastry quite thinly, and cut into 5 or 6-inch rounds. Lay a large spoonful of the filling in the centre of each round, moisten the edges of the pastry and draw them up together, sealing well. Turn the pastry over, and gently flatten it with your hand. Cut three small slits in the top centre, brush with beaten egg white and dust with caster sugar. Bake for about 15 minutes at 425°.

# Jam Tarts

8 *oz shortcrust pastry*          *jam*

Cut some rounds in the pastry with a circular cutter. Line tart or patty pans with the pastry; do not trim the paste too close to the edge. Put a piece of bread in the centre of each, or a few uncooked haricot beans, and bake blind. Remove the bread or beans, and put a generous spoonful of jam in each pastry case. Strawberry, raspberry and lemon curd seem to be the most successful. A small, baked ornament of pastry may be placed in the centre of each. Finish baking for a few minutes in a medium oven.

# Mince Pies

*rich shortcrust*          *mincemeat*

To the basic shortcrust recipe, add an extra ounce of butter and 2 teaspoons of caster sugar. Roll out the pastry fairly thinly, just under $\frac{1}{4}$ inch, the thickness of two pennies. With a pastry cutter, cut rounds to fit the patty pans. Line the pans, put a filling of mincemeat in each, and moisten the edge of the pastry. Cut tops to fit, moisten, and press the edges together, crimp with the fingers or press with a fork. Cut a small slit in the top of each pie, brush with milk glaze, and bake at 425° for 10 minutes. Reduce to 375° and bake a further 10 minutes.

179

## Chelsea Buns

18 *oz rich bread dough, using*
   *recipe for plaited tea bread*
   *on page* 167
2 *oz mixed currants and*
   *sultanas*

1 *tablespoon caster sugar*
*butter*
*egg and milk glaze*
*sugar glaze*

Roll out the dough to an oblong, 12 by 6 inches. Spread the surface thinly with softened butter. Sprinkle the fruit and sugar over the dough. Roll up as for a Swiss Roll, fairly tightly. Cut into 1-inch lengths, and put them in a square 7-inch baking tin. Glaze with egg and milk and bake in a hot oven at 450° until well risen and brown (about 20 minutes). Allow the buns to cool slightly, and brush with sugar syrup, finally dusting with caster sugar.

## Cottage Loaf

1 *lb flour*
1 *teaspoon salt*

$\frac{1}{4}$ *oz yeast*
$\frac{1}{2}$ *pint water*

Sieve the flour and salt, put into a large bowl, and warm in a gentle oven. Cream the yeast with a little warmed milk and half a teaspoon of sugar; pour into a well in the warmed flour. Leave to work in a warm part of the kitchen for about 15 minutes. Heat the water until tepid, and pour into the flour. Mix the dough together, and knead until smooth and spongy. Grease the mixing bowl, after cleaning it out, and put the dough in to rise. Brush the surface with melted butter. Knock back, and break off a piece of dough weighing roughly 4–5 oz, slightly less than half the size of the other piece. Form both pieces into rounds, or bun shapes, and place the smaller piece on top of the larger. Flour your forefinger, and push it right through the centre of both pieces to the baking sheet beneath, fixing them firmly in place. Leave to prove, and bake at 450° for 30 minutes. Lower to 375° and bake a further 20 minutes, or until well risen and brown.

# Bedfordshire Wigs, Tander Cakes and Catterns

One of Mrs Bridges' mother's recipes, from her home county. In her day, the local people celebrated the lace-makers' festival of Cattern and Tander, jumping over lighted candles, drinking hot elderberry wine, and eating Cattern Cakes and Wigs. Mrs Bridges wrote, 'My mother remembers them jumping over candles, and even through bonfires, but I never saw it, it was before my time.' What they were really celebrating was the ancient fire festival of the winter solstice, and these Bedford cakes remain as a ritual bread. But even they are no longer made in Bedfordshire.

1 lb flour
½ teaspoon salt
1 heaped dessertspoon sugar

¾ oz yeast
2 eggs
3 oz butter

Make a bread dough in the manner described in the previous recipe, but adding the beaten eggs, the butter and the sugar worked to a soft dough with warm milk instead of water. This recipe requires slightly more yeast.
(For Tander Cakes add 4 oz mixed dried fruit and the grated rind of a lemon.) Shape it into individual buns or bake as one large bun loaf. For Cattern Cake omit the fruit and add 1 oz caraway seeds then shape as a large bun loaf. Wigs are sugar buns, using the same dough, flavoured with caraway seeds. In all cases, glaze with egg and milk and bake at 425°. Glaze with sugar syrup, and sprinkle the buns with crushed loaf sugar.

# Soda Bread

1 lb flour
1 teaspoon salt
1 teaspoon bicarbonate of soda
½ oz butter

½ pint or less buttermilk
(fresh milk can be used, but
if so, add a heaped teaspoon
of cream of tartar)

Sift the flour, salt and soda into a mixing bowl. Cut in butter. Gradually add the milk to make a soft dough. Knead until smooth. Shape into a flat, circular loaf about 2 inches thick. Put the loaf on a baking sheet, and cut a cross in the top of the dough with a sharp knife, bisecting it in quarters or 'farls', as the Irish say. Bake in the oven at 425° for 35 minutes, or until the bread sounds hollow when tapped on the bottom. The bread can be baked substituting wholemeal flour for some of the white.

## Lardy Cake

1 *lb rich bread dough, using recipe for plaited tea bread on page* 167

4 *oz lard*
2 *oz currants*
*caster sugar*

Roll out the bread dough into an oblong, spread threequarters of the surface with lard, sprinkle with half the currants, and dust with a tablespoonful of sugar. Fold over the uncovered portion into the centre and fold the rest over. Press down, and turn the open end towards you. Roll out as before, spread rest of the lard, and use rest of the currants, sprinkling the same quantity of sugar. Fold as before, turn and roll. Fold one half over the other. The method used is much like the method for puff pastry or flaky pastry. You now have a cake of dough with several layers of lard, fruit and sugar. Shape this into a round cake with your hands, turning the edges under, and making sure they are well sealed. Failure to seal in the lard results in the cake opening out like an unclenching fist; the lard runs into the baking tin. Bake in an oven at 425° for 20 minutes, or until the cake has risen and browned. Brush with sugar syrup glaze. A less rich cake can be made by using the bread dough recipe for Cottage loaf on page 182.

## Dripping Spice Cake

This recipe came from Mrs Bridges' home town of Bristol, 'a recipe kindly given after many requests, by Mrs Oatby, the cook at the hotel.' We are not told which hotel, but it may have been the Grand Spa at Clifton. The cake is a solid spice and fruit cake, like bread pudding.

1 lb flour
6 oz dripping
8 oz mixed, dried fruit
6 oz brown Barbados sugar
3 eggs

½ pint milk
1 good tablespoon black treacle
1 teaspoon mixed spice
1 teaspoon bicarbonate of soda

Sift flour and spice into a bowl, and rub in the dripping until well 'taken up'. Add the sugar, the fruit and the eggs, well beaten. Warm the milk and the treacle together, add the soda, and pour into the mixture. Make a batter of dropping consistency, and pour into an 8-inch cake tin, well papered and buttered. Bake at 325° for 2½ hours, or until a skewer comes away cleanly.

## Gingerbread

'There are more different recipes for gingerbread than there are proverbs in the Bible,' writes Mrs Bridges solemnly. 'Gingerbread varies in weight, texture, flavour and appearance from village to village, town to town. It is one of the oldest and most English of all cakes. This recipe is no better or worse than any other.'

10 oz flour
8 oz Barbados sugar
6 oz butter
3 tablespoons black treacle
3 tablespoons golden syrup

1 teaspoon bicarbonate of soda
2 eggs
2 teaspoons ground ginger
2 teaspoons ground cinnamon
½ teaspoon mixed spice

Put all the dry ingredients in a mixing bowl. Warm the treacle and syrup with the butter in a pan over a low heat, stirring until the butter has melted. Blend into the flour mixture, stirring to a smooth batter. Beat the eggs and add by degrees to the batter. Pour into a prepared square cake tin, and bake in an oven set at 350° for about 30 minutes.

## Cornflour Cake

2 oz flour
2 oz cornflour
2 eggs
4 oz butter
5 oz sugar

½ teaspoon baking powder
1 tablespoon milk
vanilla flavouring or the
    grated rind of half a lemon

Cream the butter with the sugar, separate the yolks of the eggs and beat the yolks in with the butter. Sift the flour and corn-flour together, and beat into the mixture. Add the vanilla, or a little grated lemon rind, and the baking powder dissolved in the milk. Whip the egg whites stiff, and fold into the batter. Pour into a prepared 6-inch cake tin, and sprinkle a teaspoon of sugar mixed with a teaspoon of flour over the top. Bake for 1 hour at 350°.

## Rock Cakes

½ teaspoon salt
8 oz flour
4 oz butter or good dripping
4 oz sugar
4 oz currants or sultanas

1 oz candied peel
1 teaspoon baking powder
3 eggs
cream

Sift salt, flour and baking powder together, and rub in the dripping or butter. Add the sugar and the fruit. Beat the eggs and mix to a stiffish dough. If it is too stiff, add enough cream to soften it, but the appearance of true Rock Cakes depends on the dough holding its shape during baking. Divide the dough into small cakes with two forks, placing the piles on a baking sheet. Bake at 400° for 15 minutes.

## Scones

'Hudson's recipe', wrote Mrs Bridges. Hudson was the butler at Eaton Place, and he was Scottish, so presumably knew the recipe by heart. The scones were made with buttermilk, which plays an important part in the baking of breads in Wales and Ireland, as well as in Scotland. Soda and buttermilk together makes good leaven.

1 lb flour
1 teaspoon salt
2 oz butter

1 teaspoon bicarbonate of soda
½ pint buttermilk

Sift the flour with salt and the soda, rub in the butter to fine crumbs. Add the buttermilk (or fresh milk with a heaped tea-spoon of cream of tartar) and knead to a stiff dough. Flour a board and roll or press the dough to ½ or ¾ inch thick. Cut rounds with a 2 or 2½-inch pastry cutter, or with the rim of a glass tumbler. Bake for 10–15 minutes, or until they are well risen and golden brown.

## Seed Cake

10 *oz flour*
5 *oz sugar*
4 *oz butter*
1 *egg*

1 *teaspoon baking powder*
2 *teaspoons caraway seeds*
*pinch of salt*
3 *tablespoons milk*

Cream the butter and sugar, beat the egg and add to the butter, also the caraway seeds. Sift the flour with the salt and the baking powder. Fold in by degrees, and add sufficient milk to make a batter of soft dropping consistency. Pour into a prepared 8-inch cake tin, and bake on a centre shelf at 350°, for about 45 minutes. Test with a skewer, and leave to cool in the tin before turning out on a cake rack.

## Vinegar Cake

Both vinegar and ammonia were used in cakes as raising agents; mixed with bicarbonate of soda they produce carbon dioxide, which made the cake light. Neither the vinegar nor the ammonia affected the taste of the cake. Vinegar cake is a pleasant golden Madeira type of luncheon cake.

8 *oz flour*
8 *oz sugar*
8 *oz butter*
4 *eggs*
*grated peel of* ½ *lemon*

2 *tablespoons vinegar*
*scant* ½ *teaspoon bicarbonate of soda*
*nutmeg*

Cream the butter and the sugar, then add the beaten eggs by degrees. Sift flour with the soda and fold into the butter. Add the peel and a pinch of nutmeg. Have the oven set at 350°, also have ready a cake tin of 6-inch diameter, lined with buttered greaseproof paper. Pour the vinegar into the batter, stir it in well, and pour quickly into the cake tin. Level the top and put on the centre shelf of the oven. Cover with a piece of greaseproof paper, and leave for 1 hour, then remove the paper and cook a further 30 minutes, or until a skewer comes away clean.

# GLOSSARY

BAIN-MARIE: A utensil comparable to a double boiler.

BASMATTI RICE: Long-grain rice originating in India; use any good long-grain rice.

BEST END OF NECK: Rack of lamb.

BISTO: Substitute Bovril or bouillon cubes.

CASTER SUGAR: Granulated sugar (sugar that can be shaken from a caster).

CORNFLOUR: Cornstarch.

COURGETTES: Small zucchini.

DOUBLE CREAM: Heavy or whipping cream.

ESSENCE, ANCHOVY: Anchovy paste.

ESSENCE, VANILLA: Vanilla extract.

GAMMON: Smoked ham.

KNOCK BACK (DOUGH): To punch down.

MARMITE: Substitute Bovril or bouillon cubes.

NUT OF BUTTER: Small piece of butter.

OXO: Substitute Bovril or bouillon cubes.

PATNA RICE: Long-grain rice originating in India; use any good long-grain rice.

RASHER (OF BACON): Slice or strip of bacon.

RATAFIA: A small, sweet almond-paste biscuit; a liqueur flavored with fruits and bitter almond.

SILVERSIDE: Top or bottom round of beef.

SINGLE CREAM: Light or "coffee" cream.

SULTANAS: Seedless white raisins.

TAMMY (probably from Fench *tamis*): A strainer or sieve.

TREACLE: Molasses.

VEGETABLE MARROW: Large zucchini.

ZEST: Outer layer of peel (without pith) of citrus fruits—lemons, oranges, tangerines, etc.

# INDEX

191